THE POWER
OF MIRACLES

JOAN WESTER ANDERSON

THE POWER OF MIRACLES

TRUE STORIES OF GOD'S PRESENCE

LOYOLAPRESS.

CHICAGO

LOYOLAPRESS.

3441 N. ASHLAND AVENUE
CHICAGO, ILLINOIS 60657
(800) 621-1008
WWW.LOYOLABOOKS.ORG

Cover and interior design by Adam Moroschan

Cover photograph: Angel Gabriel, St. Paul's Cathedral, London, England © Patrick Corrigan

Library of Congress Cataloging-in-Publication Data
Anderson, Joan Wester.
   The power of miracles : true stories of God's presence / Joan Wester Anderson.
      p. cm.
   Includes bibliographical references (p.237) and index.
   ISBN 0-8294-2213-7 (alk. paper)
   1. Miracles. I. Title.
BT97.3.A53 2005
231.7'3—dc22

2005010878

Printed in the United States of America
05   06   07   08   09   10   Versa   10   9   8   7   6   5   4   3   2   1

CONTENTS

Acknowledgments   **vii**

Signs from God   **1**

Not My Way but Yours   **11**

What God Has Done   **21**

Nothing Is Impossible   **35**

Miracle on the Mountain   **43**

Janie's Vision   **53**

Heavenly Dream   **57**

Soldier to the Rescue   **61**

Delilah's Prayer   **67**

Guardian on the Bench   **71**

Part of the Glory   **77**

With a Little Help from Mom   **83**

The Thanksgiving Angel   **89**

Angels All around Us   **99**

Touches from Above   **109**

Mississippi Miracle   **119**

What Now, God?   **125**

Wrapped in Protection   **131**

CONTENTS

Mysterious Ways   **141**

Just in Time   **149**

To Sir, with Love   **157**

Our God Reigns   **165**

The Other Passenger   **175**

Home for Christmas   **181**

Tina's Angels   **187**

And a Little Child Shall Lead Them   **195**

Moments of Love   **209**

Heaven in Hazard   **227**

The Last Word   **233**

Recommended Reading List   **237**

Other Areas of Interest   **239**

Share Your Story   **241**

About the Author   **243**

ACKNOWLEDGMENTS

I would like to thank those who offered help and information to my writing efforts. They include those readers and friends who sent me story leads or were able to add details to pieces already written, including Celeste Shaw Sullivan, of Arlington Heights, Illinois; Ethel Lynch Caldwell, of Chicago, Illinois; Jacqueline Spierenburg, of Bradenton, Florida; Jim Bramlett, of Orlando, Florida; Barbara Gove, of Horse Shoe, North Carolina; author Michael Brown, of Palm Coast, Florida; and the gracious staffs at *Guideposts* magazine, in New York; Breakthrough Inc. in Lincoln, Virginia; and Media Fellowship International, in Bothell, Washington.

A special word of appreciation to Mother Angelica, of the Eternal Word Television Network, and Rev. J. Michael Sparough, SJ, director of Charis Ministries, who both took time to instruct me on matters involving doctrine and Bible history; as well as to Len LeSourd, of Breakthrough, who, before his 1996 death, provided some useful insights on heaven.

I'm grateful for the technical and professional assistance furnished by Julie Fitts Ritter, of the Padre Pio Foundation of America; Michele Wolford, segment producer of the television series *Could It Be a Miracle?;* personnel at the *Fayetteville (NC) Observer-Times;*

the television series *Unsolved Mysteries;* the Vineyard Christian Fellowship in Anaheim, California; the National Opinion Research Center, at the University of Chicago; the Centers for Disease Control and Prevention, in Atlanta, Georgia; and the Illinois State Police.

My thanks to film producers Albert Nader (Questar Inc.), Peter Shockey (Cascom), and Linda and Chris Lewis (Entertainment Group), whose videos have supported my efforts in researching angels, miracles, and prayers; as well as to the radio and television talk show hosts from around the country who continue to air discussions on these topics.

And, as always, special thanks go to my readers. You will never know how your constant support and willingness to share your stories with me and with one another enriches my work. You have been, and continue to be, a joyous gift.

Signs from God

*I'm thankful, Lord, that all the darkness in the world
has never put out Thy light.*

—Unknown

I was about eight when I first became aware of what a "miracle" was. In this case it involved Jesus' mother, Mary. Even though she had died a long time ago and presumably had gone to heaven, as all good people do, she also somehow had appeared to children about my age in a place across the ocean called Fátima, Portugal, to give them some messages. The apparitions had occurred in 1917, when our country was involved in the First World War (although we American Catholics did not hear about the sightings until many years later). Mary had told the children that everyone must pray for peace. If people did not, that current war would end only to have another, more serious one break out, and Russia would "spread its errors" throughout the world. The messages seemed incomprehensible to world leaders and were almost universally ignored. Just a few months after the apparitions ended, communism took hold in Russia, and the Second World War did turn out to be worse than the first.

Although the political significance was beyond my young grasp, I was fascinated by the idea that heaven and earth could intersect in this way, that Mary (or, as we called her, the "Blessed Mother") could visit earth for a particular purpose.

As I grew, I heard of other visions—some involving Mary, others with her and Jesus—offering similar messages: "God loves you. Ask for forgiveness. Amend your lives. Pray for peace." The Catholic Church is slow to investigate and accept such events as genuine (although Fátima was eventually authenticated), and news of amazing happenings in other Christian denominations were rare and usually "over there," halfway around the world in some remote area, having little influence on my daily life. I decided eventually that miracles were spectacular, sun-spinning events, bestowed on rare occasions upon special saints so the rest of us would not forget our ultimate destiny: heaven.

In the mid-1980s, however, my thinking changed. That's when our family received a miracle of its own.

I've written about it before, how our son was rescued from freezing to death on the side of a road by—there could be no other explanation—an angel disguised as a tow-truck driver, who then mysteriously disappeared. The event sent me on another quest about miracles, with new queries. If God would do this for us, just an ordinary family, would he do this, was he doing this, for others? Yes! It seemed to be a well-kept secret, but soon I found more than enough people from a wide variety of religious faiths with angel stories to contribute to a book. It was a book I titled *Where Angels Walk* that I doubted many people would read. Yet less than two years later, the popularity of angels had swept the country: talk shows featured them, stores carrying nothing but angel merchandise opened, and both *Time* and *Newsweek* devoted their Christmas covers to the subject. What was happening—was it just a new trend? In part. But, as *Time* noted, "if heaven is willing to sing to us, it is little to ask that we be willing to listen."

As angels remained popular, I noticed something else: an increase in the frequency and intensity of mystical occurrences being reported among "ordinary people." Now that the floodgates had opened, people no longer hesitated to stand up at a conference or in a church audience and give testimony to a wonderful event in their lives. As a nation, we were becoming more comfortable relating earth to heaven. Miracles were no longer uncommon and limited to saintly figures. It seemed that many of us were touching a piece of God's glory.

And accounts of miracles keep increasing. We find people bearing the stigmata (the wounds of Christ) in the United States and other countries. There are numerous reported visions of the mother of Jesus. Although her longest-running alleged appearance (daily since 1981) takes place in Medjugorje, Herzegovina, she is no longer limited to hillsides in predominantly Catholic areas but seems to be touching all cultures, appearing on a Coptic Orthodox church in Zeitoun, Egypt, and in Rwanda, Syria, and Korea. Since April 1987, on the first anniversary of the explosion in Chernobyl, as many as half a million people in Ukraine have claimed to see ongoing apparitions of her, accompanied by angels.

Nor are such messages limited to the mother of Christ. Protestant missionaries recount an amazing flow of God's Spirit in places such as Australia, Taiwan, Thailand, and the Philippines. For example, a "great miraculous outpouring of our time . . . erupted in 1971 at a Bible school in Nha Trang, South Vietnam, during the dark days of the Vietnam War," writes Paul Prather in *Modern-Day Miracles*. "Spontaneously, students began to confess their sins and to minister to each other with a tremendous sense of joy. They decided to go out witnessing about their newly charged faith. Wherever they went, miracles shot out from the Nha Trang Biblical and Theological Institute into the countryside like Roman candles. Sensational healings and exorcisms became particularly common, but there were also reports of dead bodies that resurrected through prayer."

"Spiritual signals" are also happening within religions other than Christianity. In the mid-1990s, there were four lunar eclipses over Jerusalem, all coinciding with significant Jewish holy days; in 1994, the birth of an all-white buffalo in Janesville, Wisconsin, fulfilled a Native American prophecy that portends new spiritual knowledge. About that same time, reports came from India that statues of Ganesha, the Hindu deity with the head of an elephant, had started drinking milk from spoons. Word quickly spread via phone and CNN to temples in the United States and elsewhere, as Hindus of different castes and educational backgrounds flocked by the millions to their holy places with milk. The episode lasted for little more than a day in India, and about a week in other countries, as most Indian scientists debunked it. Yet it undoubtedly drew the Hindu world's attention to spiritual matters, just as tears flowing from Greek Orthodox icons, the sun spinning at holy shrines, and other unexplainable happenings seem to do.

"Some people argue that supernatural acts reported by religions other than their own are superstitions, the results of hysteria or even hoaxes," writes Prather. "Still others hold that God is quite willing to perform miracles for people who happen not to belong to their own organization." The most recent Roman Catholic catechism states specifically that God doesn't necessarily limit his work to Christians, much less to members of particular denominations. Every person he has created is his child, and is equally loved.

But God has always loved his children. Why does he seem to be sending more miracles today than ever before? "There has never been a global outpouring of divine manifestations of this magnitude in the known history of the world," writes Janice T. Connell in *Meetings with Mary*. "[The] visionaries of Medjugorje have said that no one in the world will be excluded from the messages delivered by the Blessed

Mother. People everywhere are becoming aware of the seriousness of the times and the opportunities entrusted to humanity." Even if some of these manifestations are fraudulent or hard to interpret, such as the Hindu milk episode or oil flowing from statues, their sheer number encourages us to believe that God is sending signals to his people. He wants our love and attention because, without him, life is so much more difficult to understand and endure. He wants to be first in our hearts.

Both Gallup and Fox News polls in the summer of 2005 found that nearly 80 percent of Americans now believe in angels, the largest percentage ever. However, in many cases, heaven is meeting resistance: "For our struggle is not with flesh and blood but with the principalities, with the powers, with the world rulers of this present darkness, with the evil spirits in the heavens" (Ephesians 6:12). According to the Bible, there have always been satanic beings roaming the earth, tempting humans to turn their backs on God and to live in selfishness and sin. And this perceived recent increase in heavenly activity has no doubt generated the same level of intensity on the "other side," leading to what some call spiritual warfare, the ultimate battle for souls.

What's Ahead for America?: Christian leaders share their concerns about the spiritual state of the union.

Charisma, October 1996

Last year Americans spent more than $8 billion on hard-core videos, peep shows . . . adult cable programming . . . computer porn and sex magazines—an amount much larger than Hollywood's domestic box office receipts and larger than all the revenues generated by rock and country music recordings.

U.S. News & World Report, February 1997

Signs and Warnings: Has the Final Hour Begun?

Signs of the Times, January 1994

It doesn't take an expert to note that, despite God's attempts to reach us, there is still a lot of chaos and suffering in our world. Children weep over a broken home, teenagers find life deprived of meaning, young couples worry about finances and broken promises, the elderly grapple with disease and loneliness; and then there are wars, famine, prejudice, destruction of nature. . . . If God truly loves us, why does he allow all this to happen?

•   *Sometimes hard times occur through no fault of our own but are just a result of living in an imperfect world.* God does not send suffering to his children, but as C. S. Lewis once noted, "pain is God's megaphone." It gets our attention. When these periods come, our job is simply to endure, getting through them with the help of God and those around us. Perhaps the struggle will teach us lessons that we can use later to help others.

- *People who are attempting to move closer to God will often find obstacles in their paths.* There is a saying that "if you're not doing anything for the kingdom, Satan leaves you alone. But if you're becoming an effective soldier, you'll find yourself under attack." Members of my Wednesday night prayer group often joke that if the weather is bad, the car breaks down, or a headache develops, it will happen on a Wednesday, giving us an excuse to stay away from our two-hour prayer time and the graces and spiritual insights that might have resulted. But the Bible confirms our observation: "When you come to serve the LORD," says the book of Sirach (2:1), "prepare yourself for trials." The solution here is to persevere. Relief will come.

- *Suffering happens, too, as a result of sin, freely chosen.* Should we be surprised when children brought up on a steady diet of gross and immoral movies and television programs act out what they see? Should we be surprised when people dabble in the occult, settle problems through violence, abandon their responsibilities? One emergency-room physician told me his personal theory: If people simply lived by the Ten Commandments, we would have no health-care crisis in our country because hospitals would not need to treat those suffering from gunshot wounds, victims of spouse or child abuse, those suffering from sexually transmitted diseases or drug overdoses, and so on. Instead, hospitals could use their resources primarily for those ill with diseases.

As God continues to try to get our attention, what lies ahead? Few people believe that the current era heralds the end of the world or the Second Coming; Jesus told us no one would know the day or the hour this would occur. But will there be a repeat of what happened when the Fátima prophecies in 1917 went unheeded? Or are we heading toward some sort of worldwide moment of truth or chastisement, when God's people may have to summon the courage to take a stand and get involved in society as never before?

Perhaps. But it's possible that there are more wondrous events ahead too. One pastor had a vision in which he saw himself in a crowded football stadium. Suddenly the Holy Spirit was beside each person in the stadium. Instantly everything stopped because God was showing every person just where he or she stood on the pathway of life and eternity, in his or her relationship to God and to evil. In the vision, people began to weep just to see the glory of heaven revealed in that way—and to realize how they had or hadn't used the gifts they'd been given. And how amazing to see dignitaries from hundreds of countries standing in silent solidarity and mutual respect at Pope John Paul II's funeral. Could it be the beginning of a new kind of peace?

Whatever comes, we know that God will make *all* things—even the hardest situations—work for the good of those who love him. What an awesome time to be alive and to see how God can turn difficulties into shining moments of hope and glory!

So this is a mystery book, one without an ending. It includes people not only from the United States but from other countries who have been touched beautifully by the hand of God or one of God's angels. It also includes those who have gone through Job-like experiences, suffering, or difficulties that have challenged many of their beliefs. Yet they hung on and can testify that, despite whatever we may witness in the coming years, God will keep his promise: "If my people . . . humble themselves and pray, and seek my presence and turn from their evil ways, I will hear them from heaven and pardon their sins and revive their land" (2 Chronicles 7:14).

Not My Way but Yours

You will be my witnesses . . . to the ends of the earth.

—Acts 1:8

When Duane Miller awakened on Sunday morning, January 14, 1990, his throat was raw, his voice a bit raspy. But he barely gave it a thought. Scheduled to preach two morning services that day, he was already mentally reviewing his material. Would his congregation be consoled, informed, inspired by his words? As senior pastor of the First Baptist Church in Brenham, Texas, Duane loved God, loved to preach and sing (he had started singing professionally at the age of sixteen), and loved family life with his wife, Joylene, and their two college-age daughters. And although his church was suffering through some financial problems—which often resulted in twenty-hour workdays for Duane—his natural optimism was strong. With God on his side, what could go wrong?

Now, however, as Duane prepared for the day, he experienced that ominous stuffy, headachy, dizzy feeling that usually heralds the flu. Drinking hot tea, he managed to preach at the first service, but singing was almost impossible—even his range seemed limited to just a few notes. "During my second sermon, every sound and inflection grated on the back of my throat like sandpaper," Duane recalls. He cut his talk short, canceled the rest of his duties, and reluctantly went home to bed. Obviously, the long work hours had finally caught up with him.

The flu took almost ten days to abate. But Duane's throat did not recover. "It was painful and constricted, as if someone had my windpipe between his two fingers and was squeezing it whenever I swallowed," he explains. "There was a constant choking sensation. My voice was weak and hoarse." When Duane finally saw a physician, the throat was so swollen that the doctor could not get a scope down to examine it. Duane's nightmare had begun.

The doctor was almost certain of the diagnosis. He suspected that the flu germ had penetrated the protective sheath around the vocal cords and permanently destroyed them. Duane was probably going to live the rest of his life without a normal voice. There was the possibility, however, that the doctor's suspicions weren't correct, so he suggested Duane try some medication and visit several specialists.

When, fourteen days later, there seemed to be no real improvement with medication, Duane went to the Baylor College of Medicine in Houston for more tests. On their recommendation, he took a six months' leave of absence from his church. Perhaps his voice—his whole body—was just worn out and needed some time to recover.

Duane was discouraged during this time but not panic-stricken. After all, he was a man of faith who believed that God could and often did heal. God was obviously taking his time in answering Duane's prayers, but Duane never doubted that he, ultimately, would be healed. Hadn't God called Duane to the ministry, where speaking was absolutely essential? Despite his fears, Duane waited for God to disclose more of his always-perfect plan.

But God revealed nothing, and as time passed, new symptoms developed. Duane lost his equilibrium, and often his vision would blur. Was he going to lose his sight now as well as his voice? Life slowly became unworkable and unbearable. How could one communicate, earn a living, even take care of errands without being able to make the most minimal of sounds? Financial difficulties grew. "The mortgage company, phone company, the grocer—no one gives discounts just because you've lost your voice," Duane says. Still he believed the answers would come.

They did not. By the time the leave of absence ended, his voice hadn't improved, and the physicians offered no new diagnoses. The original diagnosis had been correct, and there was no hope of reversing the situation. Although Duane could still emit some sounds by using fatty tissue near the vocal cords, known as "false cords," these too would wear away in time. The doctors agreed that within a year or so Duane would be completely mute.

Brokenhearted, Duane resigned his pastorate. The family returned to the First Baptist Church in Houston, one of the largest church communities in the country, where he had served as pastor for twelve years prior to going to Brenham and where they had many old friends. "I faced the indignity of more medical tests, the humiliation of being without a vocational future, the anguish of watching my singing and preaching ministry being completely shut down," Duane writes in his book, *Out of the Silence.* "But I no longer faced them alone." He always had been the giver in this congregation, and now he was in need. It was not the role he would have chosen, but, for a little while, being surrounded by friends made life more bearable.

Joylene and the girls found jobs (which kept the college bills paid), Duane ran an agency that allowed him to work on paper rather than with his voice, and the family managed to rent a house they all liked very much. And when some physicians were almost positive that Duane had multiple sclerosis, the final test result was negative. In the midst of the agony, there was always just a trace of hope.

Duane was fully aware that people suffered handicaps and physical pain far more crippling than his. And yet his voice was essential to the job he had always assumed God had called him to do. What had changed? Did God now find him unworthy? "The anguish of my physical impairment began to bludgeon my spiritual life as well," Duane recalls. "If I hear anyone who goes through a trying test say he or she never doubted God, I think that person is either lying or has lost touch with reality." *What are you doing, God? Don't you love me anymore? Have you abandoned me?* How many people throughout history, both famous and obscure, have struggled with these questions? Duane Miller was no exception.

By now, because his condition was so rare, Duane was a medical celebrity. At one seminar in Switzerland, specialists from all over the world examined photos of his throat. "From the very beginning, everything had been recorded and documented, like time-lapse photography," he explains, "because every time I went to see any doctor, he would put the scope down my throat and photograph the changes, especially the growing scar tissue."

It was as if God wanted everything officially recorded so that everyone would see that the glory, when it came, was all his.

During the past three agonizing years, Duane had learned to make himself heard by forcing air through his throat and screaming at the top of his lungs. Then someone from the congregation found a microphone that, when pressed against Duane's lips, could amplify these sounds. This opened up a new possibility: perhaps Duane could occasionally teach his former Sunday school class at First Baptist. He was hesitant. Who would want to sit through such uncomfortable sounds? But his friends encouraged him, and, once in a while, he preached a short lesson.

He was doing just that on the morning of January 17, 1993, having been persuaded to substitute at the last minute for another teacher. The class was also being tape-recorded, a routine practice. The two hundred or so attendees knew about Duane's voice. But because Duane had always tried to keep his more personal problems to himself, no one in the audience was aware that he had recently lost his job and his medical insurance, had a book proposal rejected (not because of his writing ability but because he would not be physically able to do any media promotion), or that he was nearing the time when the doctors believed he would become completely mute—in short, that he was as low as he had been since the beginning of his ordeal. Nor had Duane selected that particular day's lesson, based on Psalm 103, because the series had been prescheduled. "I was feeling no great faith—in fact, inside I was still asking God, 'Why have you punished me this way?'"

In Psalm 103, the psalmist reminds us not to forget the gifts of God,

> Who pardons all your sins,
>   heals all your ills,
> Delivers your life from the pit . . .
>   your youth is renewed like the eagle's.

These were hard concepts for Duane to discuss. He truly believed that God does such things, but everyone in the congregation had watched Duane struggle for three years; they knew that God had not healed or renewed their beloved friend, despite his courage and goodness. How effective a teaching could this be?

Duane spoke for more than twenty minutes before reaching these particular verses, and he was just about ready to cut the lesson short—his throat was hurting terribly, and the strain of pushing the words out was so great that he wondered if anyone could hear him anyway—but he forged on. Reflecting on the "pit"—where he felt he was now, in a pit with no way out—he said, "I have had, and you have had, pit experiences." On the word *pit,* Duane felt something odd. The "fingers" that had been locked around his throat for three years seemed to let go! People looked up—what had happened? Duane sounded different.

Duane noticed it too. His voice was stronger, less hoarse. "Now . . . to say God doesn't do miracles today is to put God in a box, and God doesn't like to be put in a box," he said. Then he stopped, stunned. He could hear himself! His voice was normal!

Joylene left her chair in the audience and ran up to the stage. "I don't . . . understand this right now," Duane said without the microphone. "In fact, I'm at a loss for words!" He put his arms around Joylene and began to weep. Some in the congregation broke into tears; some cheered, laughed, and praised God.

Others dashed out of the room to find the senior pastor. "Duane's been healed!" they shouted.

Could it be true? "I wanted to laugh, cry, sing, shout, dance, and hug everyone I could, all at the same time," Duane recalls. "After a few brief minutes, I thought, what better way to celebrate the restoration of my voice than to teach God's word?" So he continued the lesson. And at the end of the session, the congregation burst into the most appropriate of all endings, the doxology "Praise God, from whom all blessings flow." "I don't think anyone who was there that day will ever sing the doxology in a casual manner again," Duane says. "The truth of its simplicity struck our hearts for eternity."

Word, of course, had started to spread. Dr. John Bisagno, senior pastor of the church, was conducting the scheduled worship service in the main church and now summoned Duane to the platform. People who had attended the early service had heard about Duane's restored voice, so there was standing room only in the worship center as Dr. Bisagno approached the pulpit.

"You all know Duane Miller," Dr. Bisagno began. "He's been around here for the better part of twenty years. And most of you know the problem he has had with his voice these past three years. I want him to come and tell you what God has done in his life."

Duane approached the pulpit. "Well, I'll try," he said. At that, some five thousand people jumped to their feet and began to worship God much as Duane's class had done. Some wept, some laughed, others clapped; many fell to their knees, and tears flowed freely. The organist began to play the Bill Gaither chorus "Let's Just Praise the Lord." And everyone did.

Since his healing, Duane has been back to many physicians for reevaluation, and every photo taken of his throat since January 17, 1993, shows a complete lack of scar tissue on his vocal cords. They are as smooth and healthy as they were before his tribulation began, with absolutely no indication that any problem ever existed. "Even if you could explain the coincidence of my suddenly being able to speak," Duane says, "you have to understand that scar tissue doesn't disappear by itself. What happened to it?"

And yet, after much thought, Duane is convinced that this is the central message of his entire experience. Scar tissue *does* disappear—at least the spiritual kind. God has said that he will perform glorious works for his children, and what could be more glorious than knowing that our lives, with all their failures and mistakes, can be completely restored in an instant, through his love and grace?

Nor should the very public aspect of Duane's miracle be overlooked. Not only did the witnesses in his congregation and throughout Houston experience a deepening of their faith, but word spread throughout the world as well, primarily because the entire event had been tape-recorded. So often, miracles are private, tender in their intimacy. But in this case, God had unleashed the tongues of thousands, all eager to share this good news. "God healed me not because I earned it, deserved it, had enough people praying, or any of those other reasons," Duane says, "but because he wanted people to be drawn to him and to give him all the glory." To further that cause today, while serving as senior pastor at the First Baptist Church in Bellaire, Texas, Duane is also the executive director of NuVOICE Ministries, a group committed to the church through speaking, teaching, presenting seminars, consulting, and praying.

Many believe that this is just the beginning of the glory God is going to reveal to his people in the coming years. Our God—yours, mine, and Duane's—is truly an awesome God.

WHAT GOD HAS DONE

Will doctors soon tell us,
"Say two prayers and call me in the morning"?
—ASSOCIATED PRESS, DECEMBER 6, 1995

Duane Miller was healed of a physical condition. But that's not the only way God is healing today.

For example, an "angel" who let me know about a very special healing is Jim McNamara of Mokena, Illinois. Years ago, Jim worked for Sears, Roebuck in the Chicago area, and his job involved calling upon people in their homes. "I had found the Lord, in a big way," Jim says, "so from time to time, I'd witness about him to customers, if they seemed open to it."

One day Jim had an appointment with an older couple, Mr. and Mrs. Sam Lynch, who lived on Chicago's South Side. They were warm and hospitable, and Jim liked them immediately. "After we concluded our business," Jim recalls, "I noticed a huge Bible lying on their coffee table. 'That's a very important book, isn't it?' I asked the couple."

They both nodded. "It certainly is."

Briefly, Jim told them about how he had come to know Jesus. When he had finished, Louise Lynch nodded to her husband. "Tell him what happened to you, Sam," she said.

"Well," Sam said shyly, "I'm a carpenter. And one day I felt the Lord asking me to build a church for him. And so I did."

"You did? A whole church?" Jim was astounded.

"Well, I subcontracted some of the work. But I did the plans, and most of the labor. It's still open today. The LeClaire Missionary Baptist Church, on South Lavergne Street. My name is even in a piece of the concrete wall." Sam sat back.

But there was more to the story. "Tell him what happened after it was built," Louise prodded.

Sam squirmed in his chair. Apparently, this part was harder to relate. "When they were making plans to dedicate the church, the deacons and people wanted me to read the Bible from the pulpit," Sam explained. "I kept saying no, but they kept asking."

"Why didn't you want to read?" Jim asked.

The Lynches looked at each other. "He couldn't," Louise said softly. "Sam had been illiterate his whole life. In fact, my mother originally forbade me to marry him because he couldn't read. She didn't think he would amount to anything."

The couple had eventually wed, but they had always kept Sam's disability a secret. No one ever knew about it except the three Lynch children, who, as they grew, would read to their father from newspapers and books. Sam had a quick mind and a marvelous memory, so no one ever guessed his secret. But now, if people from the new congregation kept pressuring Sam, perhaps he would have to admit it. Neither he nor Louise was happy about that.

Louise came up with a solution. "We'll choose some verses," she told Sam. "And I'll read them over and over to you, and you'll memorize them. Then you can stand up at the pulpit, and it will look like you're reading. No one will ever know."

Sam relented. "We practiced pretty hard, every night," he told Jim. "But the verses were short, and no one knew what I was planning to read anyway, so I figured I could get through it."

The morning of the dedication came, and the church was full. Louise was sitting in the first row, and she watched proudly as Sam ascended the steps to the pulpit, picked up the open Bible, and began to read. And then her heart seemed to stop.

Sam was not reciting the verses they had practiced together. Nor was he repeating anything that remotely resembled material he knew or was familiar with. No, instead he was *reading*—loudly, confidently, even turning pages.

Jim, enthralled by the Lynches' story, asked, "How did the people in the audience react?"

"They didn't know anything special was going on," Louise answered. "Since no specific material had been planned, they just assumed Sam was reading what he had selected. He went on and on. I don't think he even fully realized what was happening."

"I didn't," Sam added. "Not until I got home, and the whole impossible situation hit me. Then I picked up a book—just to see if the whole thing had been some big mistake. And you know what? I could still read."

For the rest of his life Sam read, although sometimes a little slowly. Eventually he engaged a tutor, who came to the house and helped him progress even more. But he and Louise never forgot the marvel of that special day in church.

"God healed the blind man," Jim McNamara says. "He said, 'Lazarus, come out!' And he must have said, 'Sam, read my Scriptures.' What a God we serve!"

A woman named Margaret approached my table at a book signing with another example of healing. "I had gone to our big shopping mall for a job interview, and during that time put my two- and three-year-old girls in the babysitting service the stores provided," she explained. "Now the interview was over, and I was standing at the top of the escalator in my suit and high heels, looking down three floors through all that chrome and glass, and feeling a bit disoriented." With her left arm, she was carrying her two-year-old, her purse, and a rather heavy diaper bag. With her right hand,

Margaret was attempting to pull her three-year-old, Tammy, onto the escalator.

But Tammy was afraid to step on the moving stairs. "Mommy, I don't want to go!" she shrieked. At any moment Margaret was going to lose her grip or her balance. "I was already a very nervous mother, someone who saw danger almost everywhere. Right now I was working up to a panic. How were we going to get down safely?"

No one seemed to be near them, but then Margaret saw a firm hand come down on Tammy's shoulder. The hand belonged to a dapper, white-haired elderly gentleman wearing a dark suit. "He had smiling eyes," Margaret recalled. "Even though I was almost paranoid about strangers being near the girls, I felt comfortable with him right away."

The man eased Tammy onto the escalator and nodded at Margaret, as if to say, "I'm holding your little girl. She won't fall."

Margaret nodded back, thanking him without words.

The ride down was over in seconds, and during the flurry of getting her daughters off the escalator, Margaret lost sight of her elderly helper. Although he had been behind them and, to her recollection, hadn't stepped around them, he had vanished. There was no one matching his appearance anywhere around the sparsely populated mall, not even walking away from them. Where had the helpful stranger gone?

"Tammy," she asked, "did you see where that man went?"

Tammy looked up. "What man, Mommy?"

"The man on the escalator. The one who put his hand on your shoulder so you wouldn't fall."

Tammy looked puzzled. "There wasn't any man on the escalator, Mommy. There was just us."

In a sudden burst of comprehension, Margaret realized she had been given a glimpse of Tammy's guardian angel—and a message. Now, infused into her spirit were words that had seemed to accompany that long look she and the elderly man had exchanged.

"As you see me now, with my hand on your child," he had somehow told her, "I am, *always.* So there is no need to be so anxious. You cannot add one day to your child's life by worrying, or take one away that is not already in God's plan. But what you can do, what you *must* do, is love your children, with the kind of love only a mother can give, for however long they have been placed in your care. This is your most important job."

"In an instant," Margaret told me, "I was healed of my fear, my constant worry over every aspect of my daughters' lives. And I remain so to this day. I'm concerned and watchful, but not panicky—and there's a big difference."

No ordinary encounter could have brought such a profound and instant emotional healing, Margaret said. She had been touched ·by a messenger of God.

Sister Maurella Schlise, a Catholic nun from Fargo, North Dakota, had served others in many ways, primarily as a teacher and a hospital chaplain, but never as a prison visitor—not until one Christmas, when she traveled, as she usually did for the holidays, to the Florida home of her sister and brother-in-law, Rosemary and Pat Ryan. The Ryans had started a prison ministry, conducting weekly nondenominational prayer meetings at a nearby maximum-security penitentiary. Usually, no more than thirty-five men attended, but Rosemary and Pat refused to become discouraged. If, for just a little while, prayer lifted these prisoners out of despair and regret and focused them on the One who loved them despite it all, then the hours Rosemary and Pat donated were well worth it.

Visitors were never allowed to bring anything to the prison, not even food. But when Sister Maurella arrived at the Ryans' house, she found them preparing food not just for the family but for the prisoners too. "Because our regular prayer meeting falls on Christmas Eve this year, the prison officials decided we could bring each of the men a few 'goodies,'" Rosemary explained to Sister Maurella. "We're going to make some Rice Krispies bars and homemade cookies for them, enough to fill about fifty bags."

"Fifty bags! I thought you said the turnout was pretty low," Sister Maurella pointed out.

"It usually is. But on Christmas Eve, maybe some extra men will come. We wouldn't want to run out of food. Besides, for most, this will be their only gift."

The following morning Sister Maurella attended Mass. She thought about the inmates, wondering if they, if anyone, could actually experience the miracle of Christmas behind bars. What would it be like? Then, "although God is not in the habit of speaking directly to me," she says, smiling, "I distinctly heard a voice in my spirit. It specifically said, 'Bring one hundred bags of candy and cookies to the prison.'"

One hundred. It seemed far too many for this small group. "I thought it might be my imagination," Sister says. "But then I decided to step out in faith and tell Rosemary and Pat about it."

Rosemary and Pat were skeptical. But they, too, had experienced God seeming to nudge them just a little, and they respected Sister Maurella's insight. If Sister was wrong, the worst that could happen would be some bags left over, and at Christmas there were always plenty of places to donate extra sweets!

The women spent Christmas Eve doing many chores, as well as filling one hundred white bags with homemade treats and candy. "The men will be pleased, I think," Rosemary mused. "Each will be happy to have a little gift all his own."

After dinner, they loaded the car and drove to the prison gates. The guards waved them through. Sister Maurella looked around. So this was what a penitentiary looked like. Now someone was hurrying toward them. "That's the chaplain," Rosemary explained.

"The chapel is filled!" the chaplain called. "I've never seen it so crowded. There must be almost a hundred men inside!"

A hundred! Rosemary and Sister Maurella smiled at each other. The little nudge from heaven had been real after all. How glad they were that they had acted on it and prepared extra food.

Pat carried the box of white bags into the chapel, planning to begin the meeting in the usual way. But the prisoners had a surprise for them: They had prepared their own Christmas program. An inmate with a vibrant voice sang the moving story of the Little Drummer Boy. Another performed the "Ave Maria," having somehow discovered that it was one of Rosemary's favorites. Everyone sang hymns, and one man read the Christmas story from the Bible. The chapel was hushed, with small candles providing the only light. It was truly the most poignant Christmas Eve service that Sister had ever attended.

Finally the program ended, and the men eagerly lined up. Sister Maurella and Rosemary handed each one a white bag. "Thank you, Sister; thank you, Mrs. Ryan," they murmured, until the bags were gone. But ten men still stood in line. There had not been one hundred men in the chapel. There had been one hundred and ten.

One hundred and ten! Sister Maurella was distraught. If God had truly spoken to her, why hadn't he told her to bring one hundred and ten bags? What should they do? *God, multiply the bags,* Rosemary prayed silently.

A young convict noticed their predicament. "Sister," he spoke quietly, "we others, we'll share our bags with them."

Sister Maurella looked at the faces surrounding her: men of every color and nationality, murderers and thieves—but men who now, because of Jesus' birthday, were willing to reach out to one another in forgiveness and love. Healing sometimes came in tiny steps, she knew. Once begun, it could grow.

The young convict opened his bag, preparing to divide his sweets. Just then, a prison trustee entered the chapel, carrying a sack. "Rosemary, we had some leftovers from a group that came this morning," he said. "Can you use them?"

Rosemary took the sack. Inside were candy and cookies— divided into ten white bags.

The group was astonished. "You see?" Rosemary smiled as she handed the bags to the remaining men. "Our God loves us so much that he cares for us in even the smallest ways."

As the remaining men received their treats, everyone rejoiced— especially Sister Maurella. She had wondered if Christmas could come in a prison, and now she knew. Where love is, God is.

Although born and raised Catholic, Mary Wayman had, for a variety of reasons, been away from her church for more than ten years. "I tried a few other denominations but never got very comfortable with them and didn't join anywhere," she says. So she was a bit surprised last year when a longtime friend who was an active Catholic handed her a medal of the Virgin Mary and Child. Her friend explained that a woman in her church traveled frequently to the shrine at Medjugorje, Herzegovina, and took various items there to be blessed by the Virgin. This was one of those blessed medals. Although Mary knew that the medal had no power on its own and was only a symbol of the Blessed Virgin and her concern for her children, she was touched that her friend had thought to give it to her, someone who didn't even go to a Catholic church. She started carrying the medal in her pocket every day.

Mary is a horsewoman and has owned several horses over the years. Recently she had purchased a mare named Abby who was, she had decided, the best horse she had ever owned. "We just fit together—I loved her." On a freezing Sunday afternoon a few weeks after Mary received the medal, she drove to the boarding stable where she kept Abby. "I walked out to the pasture and brought her into the barn to check on a problem she'd been having with her feet," Mary says. "She didn't act like herself at all; she wouldn't even take a treat from me, and all horses love treats. After watching her for a while, it was becoming obvious that she was in the beginning stages of colic."

The word *colic* strikes fear in the hearts of horse owners; the illness is probably the single biggest killer of horses. Mary called her veterinarian, who came immediately and agreed that Abby's colon was not functioning as it should. If a horse's colon becomes twisted, its blood supply is cut off, and the colon stops working for lack of circulation—and that means certain death for the horse.

For the rest of the afternoon and into the evening, Mary and the barn owner kept Abby under surveillance, doing whatever they could to make her well. Around 10:00 p.m., they phoned the vet again. When he came by, the news was not good: Abby was worse than she had been on his first visit. He gave her another injection for the pain.

Just then Mary remembered the medal in her pocket. It had been there all along, but she hadn't thought to ask heaven for a healing for Abby. Did people do such things for animals, especially people like her—someone who hadn't been giving God a lot of attention lately? Was she worthy to pray?

But God had said he would listen to anyone. Now Mary stood, holding the medal tightly, and pleaded for a miracle. "I then placed the medal on Abby's left side and prayed that her colon resume functioning. I walked around to the other side and did the same thing." A few moments later, Mary and the barn manager ran into the house to get warm. While there, they heard Abby thrashing. "We found her lying in her stall, convulsing with pain and unable to stand. We called the vet again."

The three of them managed to get Abby up and out of her stall. Her pulse rate had skyrocketed. Her gums were gray, and now there were no sounds in her colon. "The vet looked at me with the saddest expression," Mary says. "We both knew that this beautiful mare wasn't going to make it. We had to decide where to take her"—when horses are euthanized, they must be brought to the spot where they will be buried, if possible, because they are so large and heavy—"and finally decided on an area where the barn keeper's horse had been buried last spring."

So in minus-ten-degree weather, the barn keeper, the vet, and Mary slowly walked Abby to the place where she would receive her final injection.

Just as they were getting ready to do so, however, Abby's head shot up. She whinnied to the horses back in the barn and began rooting around in the snow for something to eat!

"Let me check her again," said the doctor in disbelief. A moment later he was shaking his head. "Her pulse rate has dropped back to normal. I can hear sounds in her colon too."

Mary was afraid to hope. Was it just a false alarm? Once they returned to the barn the doctor checked the horse's gums, only to find that now they were bright pink!

Mary watched Abby all night long for signs of her illness returning, but it never did. "I have absolutely no doubt that my prayers resulted in a miracle that saved Abby's life," Mary says. "She had been too far gone for any other explanation. Needless to say, my faith has been fully restored, and I'll never doubt in the power of prayer or God ever again. I wear the medal on a silver chain around my neck every day."

The visionaries at Medjugorje have been told that glories will be experienced all over the world, by people of all faiths, as a result of the Virgin Mary's appearances there. No one has specifically mentioned horses being healed.

But why not?

Nothing Is Impossible

My God, how wonderful thou art,
Thy majesty how bright!
—F. W. Faber, "The Eternal Father"

God has promised his people dominion over the entire earth, as long as we respect it all. The great Episcopalian mystic Agnes Sanford, after asking God if it was permissible to pray for sunshine, would pray specifically to stop a storm, and dramatic things would often happen. Most of us wouldn't even think about asking for such things. But Nel van Schaik Roeleveld has tried it—and she believes.

Nel grew up in Nazi-occupied Holland, where life was extremely difficult, but her close-knit family always believed God was looking out for them. One evening, it was Nel's turn to set the table for dinner, although, as she well knew, there was not a bit of food in the house. "What should I do, Daddy?" she asked.

"Set the table anyway, and we'll pray" was his reply.

As the family began the Our Father, they heard a loud knock at the front door. Frightened that it might be soldiers, Nel followed her father as he answered the summons. A stranger was standing outside, holding the biggest loaf of fresh-baked bread that Nel had ever seen. "I have orders to deliver this to you, Mr. Van Schaik," the man announced, "and a very good evening to you!"

Astonished, the family gave thanks not only for the bread but for the faith they shared.

That faith, however, in the Reformed Church, was also a source of confusion for Nel. She was being raised to believe that God had two official books. In one were the names of those people predestined to go to hell; in the other, the names of those selected for heaven. "No one could alter anything in this setup—it stood fixed and finished. I was told to be a good girl, and when I died, I would discover where I belonged." This theory didn't seem right, the child thought. But who was she to question it?

Eventually the Van Schaiks immigrated to Pretoria, South Africa, where they attended the Afrikaans-speaking Reformed Church. Nel met and married her husband, G. J. (Roelie) Roeleveld, and the couple had three children. "We remained active in the Reformed Church," Nel relates. "But as time passed, we felt less comfortable there. Roelie and I were repeatedly accused of being 'not good Christians' because we sent our children to English-speaking schools. This shook us a bit, because we could not imagine God having likes or dislikes regarding nationality and language."

Nel began to long for real answers about God. One night she had a dreamlike experience. Someone, a gentle fatherly figure, was standing by her bedside. He bent low so Nel could see his face. It was full of goodness, holiness, and strength, and he seemed to know her very well. Nel was filled with joy and recognition. "Are you the Lord?" she asked.

Somehow, he conveyed to her that he was. He put his hand on her forehead in a gesture of blessing, and did the same to her husband sleeping next to her. Blissfully Nel fell into a sound sleep.

She told no one of her experience. "But a ray of light, like a laser beam, had penetrated my thinking," she says. "Perhaps there was more to be known about Christianity than I had ever thought possible." She began to pray that God guide her to a church community that would nourish her and teach her more about him.

Eventually, Nel and her family joined an English-speaking Methodist church, where the hymns and teachings stirred her heart. "Here I learned that God kept only one book, in which names of many people were written down, and there was room for everybody," she says. "Every time a name was added, God and his angels rejoiced. Yet the book contained many blank pages. This was because, before your name could be added, you had to make a personal decision to follow the Lord all the way."

As time passed, Nel made that decision. She read the Bible and worked more diligently to correct her faults. She and her husband and children were all baptized, and the family visited Pentecostal church services to learn more about the gifts of the Holy Spirit. The family began to pray in tongues, which deepened everyone's prayer life. At times, Nel felt she was being readied for some kind of mission. But what? And why would God choose a housewife living in a small village in South Africa—seemingly at the ends of the earth—to work for him? Nel had sought God almost completely by herself. But now she needed a definite answer from above. Was she on the right path? Did he have a specific job for her? "God, give me a sign," Nel often prayed.

At this point, Nel's older daughter, Charlotte, wanted a bedroom of her own. "We had a little storeroom available in a corner of the house," Nel says. "Roelie added a window to it, and Charlotte was happy with it."

Until winter came. Then, two walls in the storeroom began to glisten with water. "I had forgotten that these walls had leaked from rain and condensation for the seven years we'd been in the house. It hadn't mattered so much when it was a storeroom." But now she needed two huge towels to wipe down the walls each morning. Nel thought there must be a better way.

Was this the kind of thing she should ask God about? Or was it so small that it would insult the magnificence of the Almighty?

Why should he be concerned with her water problem? And yet, Nel remembered the loaf of bread so unexpectedly delivered when she was a child, and the vision of Love himself that she had received one night as she slept.

Nel knelt down by Charlotte's bed. She would mention the walls briefly, she decided. But "while praying, I was astonished by an awareness of a Presence standing to my left, just inside the room," she remembers. "Somehow the Presence told me to actually put my hands on those walls, and to pray over them using my new tongue language."

Was it an angel? The request seemed so odd. Was she imagining things? She started to pray timidly again: "Lord, you can fix the walls, and they do need fixing . . ."

Again, she sensed the same message. God wanted her to participate in his work, to take authority over problems with confidence. *Get up and go to the wall.* Nel considered that she *was* alone, and no one would know what she was about to do. She went and placed her hands on the walls, touching them in several places. "I commanded them to dry up in the name of Jesus," she says. "Then I prayed in my tongue language, thanked the Lord for this miracle, and hung the wet towels outside to dry."

The next morning, as she entered Charlotte's room, Nel held her breath. "I went up to the walls, felt them, looked—then stared. The walls were perfectly dry." Nel pulled Charlotte's bed away from the walls. The area behind the bed was dry as well.

Nel said nothing to her family. What if the whole thing was a coincidence? The following day the family left on vacation for several weeks. When they arrived back in the pouring rain, they met their neighbor. "I hope you had nice weather," he said, "because here it has been raining steadily every day for two weeks."

Charlotte's room would be flooded, Nel thought as she hurried into the house, leaving a trail of holiday baggage in her wake. But no. Astonished, she gazed at the walls—they were completely dry, as if they had been bathed in two weeks of sunshine instead of streaming rainwater.

On another occasion, after she had put her then infant son Martin to bed in his crib in her room, Nel needed to get a sweater from her closet. Not wanting to turn on a light and awaken him, Nel felt her way in the darkness, retrieved the sweater, and was almost out the door when she heard a strange rasping sound coming from the baby's crib.

Instantly Nel switched on a light and noticed that baby Martin seemed to be having trouble breathing.

The rattle! Where was the baby's rattle? Trying not to panic, Nel found the little plastic toy under the baby's blanket and saw that there was a thin, jagged-edged piece missing from it. The baby must have swallowed it! Forcing herself to remain composed, Nel pried open Martin's mouth, but she could see nothing. And yet, the baby's raspy breathing continued. It must be stuck much farther down than she could see.

By now, Martin's skin was turning an unhealthy purple hue, and he was beginning to choke. "Lord," Nel cried out, "what do I do? How do I pray?"

Take authority. Again, she remembered. God had not left his children helpless in this world. He had given them dominion over all things, if they would but pray that his power be given to them. A calmness came over her as she reached for the baby and put him in a sitting position. Then she spoke, with strength, to that fragment of plastic. "In the name of Jesus, come out of my baby now. Come out!"

Immediately, Martin let out a huge burp, and something red appeared in his mouth. Was he bleeding? No, it was the piece of missing plastic! She opened Martin's mouth, took out the plastic, gave the baby a drink, and put him back to sleep.

"No, Charlotte's little room did not become a shrine," Nel says today. "But it never leaked again." Nor did baby Martin suffer any ill effects from what could have been a tragedy. And Nel, who had come face-to-face with the results of acts of faith, had no doubt that God was going to use her in his work, again and again, whenever she asked. Today she and Roelie lead a busy and spiritually based life helping others, with plenty of time for prayer. All that is needed to work in God's kingdom, she has learned, is a willing heart—and the courage to ask for miracles.

MIRACLE ON THE MOUNTAIN

[Miracles] are designed with one goal in mind:
to bring glory to God.
—JODIE BERNDT, *CELEBRATION OF MIRACLES*

Healings, inner stirrings, challenges to our faith, warnings, even visions and dreams—God communicates with us in many ways. Jackie Greaves knows this very well.

When she and two male friends set off to climb the nearly four-thousand-foot Derry Cairngorm, one of Scotland's highest mountain peaks, where conditions can sometimes be as treacherous as those of the Himalayas, Jackie was far from intimidated. Rather, the fifty-two-year-old school secretary and grandmother from Warrington, England, was looking forward to the venture. She had hiked mountains for many years but hadn't done much climbing until recently. Yet she was always careful and well prepared. For this trip, she had packed a rucksack containing emergency food and some survival supplies and had dressed warmly. Her companions, both teachers at the school where she worked, were younger and even more experienced than she. What could go wrong?

The trio biked up the hilly terrain for the first three miles, then chained the bikes and continued on foot. It was a typical cold, clear Sunday in February 1994, and despite the exertion, Jackie felt exhilarated. There's something to be said for conquering the elements, she thought. With any luck, they'd soon be at the top of this peak!

They had just stopped to share some sandwiches, about 2:00 p.m., when gale-force winds seemed to come from nowhere. "They whipped up the snow, creating a whiteout, and we could hardly see our hands in front of our faces," Jackie says. The three knew they had to get back to safety as soon as possible. Carefully, they started to turn—then suddenly, the cliff on which they were standing gave way! In a cloud of snow, Jackie's companions vanished. Screaming, Jackie herself hurtled down the side of the wall.

"The fall was terrifying, and it seemed to go on for ages," she says. "I was holding my ice ax, and I managed to swing it into the side of the cliff as I was falling." The ice caught the ax, pulling it out of her hands but slowing her tumble, and she managed to dig her heels into the slippery side of the mountain. She had stopped!

Slowly Jackie scraped out enough snow to make a hole and wriggled into a sitting position inside. The blizzard was still too heavy for her to see anything. Jackie was alive—bruised but uninjured, as far as she could tell—but where was she? Because she had fallen so far, she surmised that she was right above a plateau. "Dave!" she shouted. "Bruce, are you there?" No response came except the whistle of the wind.

Then the whiteout cleared for just a moment, and Jackie's terror increased. She wasn't anywhere near a plateau. No, beneath her were hundreds of feet of . . . nothing. She was hanging almost vertically to the side of this precipice. Any moment, her precarious position could give way, and she would crash downward again, perhaps to her death.

The whiteout closed around her once more. Jackie sat there as an hour passed, perhaps two. Occasionally she blew her whistle, the distress signal, but no one responded. She had never felt so alone in all her life, except for the tragic period six years ago when her eighteen-year-old daughter, Lesley, had died in a car accident. That was when Jackie turned away from God. Admittedly, she had never been a very spiritual person. But there was no reason to pray to Someone who would let such a wonderful person as Lesley die.

Now, however, as the snow whirled about her, Jackie wished she had faith. Maybe God would listen after all.

Wait! Jackie looked up. Was that a light above her? Yes, a light white and clear, shining as a flashlight beam through the now-darkening mist. Was another climber coming to rescue her? "Bruce! Dave! Here I am!" Jackie shouted and frantically blew her whistle.

No one answered, nor did the light move. But as night fell and the snow continued to blow, the warm inexplicable glow remained.

On Sunday evening at 9:00, eight police officers, fourteen volunteers, and a helicopter on standby assembled at the base of the Cairngorm Mountains, alerted by Jackie's friend Bruce, who had managed to reach help. They would split into two groups and start their climb, looking for Dave and Jackie. "If they're dressed warmly enough, and not injured, they may survive," one rescuer told another.

"Right," the other responded. "Unless this blizzard keeps up."

The blizzard kept up. For seventeen hours, Jackie lay at an angle against the side of the mountain, too frightened to move, while sixty-mile-an-hour winds buffeted her slight figure. Her body shivering and her teeth chattering, she reviewed her life and thought about her two remaining children and her beloved grandchildren. She ate snow and wished she felt secure enough to open her knapsack and put on her remaining clothes. But if she slipped . . . Terror rose in her. Then it subsided, and calm once again moved over her: there was no need to panic, for she was not alone. Hundreds of feet above her, like a watchful beacon, the mysterious light continued to shine. Where had it come from? And why did it stay?

About 6:00 a.m., as the area around her grew brighter, Jackie realized that the beam was dimming. Soon it disappeared. She was still wrapped in whirling snow, stiff and frozen, but during these desolate hours on the side of the mountain, she had come to a decision. She could either die here, waiting for rescuers who would probably never find her, or she could risk climbing farther down and possibly falling. "I hacked a place in the ice with my toe, slid down on my stomach, hacked another place with the other foot, and decided to keep going," she says. Her plan worked. By 7:30 a.m., she had reached the plateau, piled high with snowdrifts, far beneath her. She managed to open the frozen zipper on her knapsack and pull on the extra clothing she had brought. But what now? The cold was terrible, the wind still fierce. There was white above her, white beneath her—in what direction should she go?

It was impossible. She couldn't go anywhere or make any more decisions, not without God. She had tried so long to ignore him, but it just hadn't worked. "God," she heard herself say, "I don't know why this is happening, or where I'm going, but you're my only hope. Please don't leave me."

Then something strange happened. She thought she heard some-one calling, a man's voice. But it was coming from far below her. How could that be—wasn't she at the bottom of the mountain by now? It must be her imagination. Struggling against the gusts and the drifts taller than she was, Jackie painfully put one foot in front of the other, again and again. *God, don't leave me. Don't leave me. . . .*

She had been walking for hours, it seemed, when she heard it: *Stop.* It was almost a whisper, a dream word, but not quite. Why, there was a barrier in front of her. Jackie squinted against the white surroundings. It was a railroad-crossing bar! But that was impossible—there were no railroad tracks here. Jackie leaned to touch it, and it disappeared. Was she hallucinating?

But wait! Jackie almost screamed. A huge hole lay ahead of her, right where she had almost stepped. She could see down into it, hundreds of feet below. She *wasn't* at the bottom of the mountain, as she had presumed. No, she was on another ledge, and she could plunge through it, just as she had done earlier.

Terror-stricken, Jackie turned to her right and took a step. Immediately, a second railroad barrier slid down right in front of her. Again she stopped, and the barrier vanished. Beyond where it had been she saw another wide hole.

Turning, Jackie went back the way she had come. She felt a strong Presence. Someone was definitely with her. Someone had just saved her from death.

It had been a long, frustrating day, Willie Fraser decided as he and Solo, his German shepherd, drove home. Daunting weather conditions had forced one of last night's search parties to dig in and remain on the mountaintop, but his team had searched until dawn. They had found the other man safe and well, and that was something to be grateful for. But they had not found Mrs. Greaves. (The searchers did not yet know that Jackie's companions, disoriented by the whiteout, had given the rescue teams incorrect directions as to where she might be.)

Willie and Solo, along with seventy others, had searched for almost ten hours that day. At one point, Willie had glanced up through the whirling snow to a plateau just above him and thought he saw something moving. But when he shouted, the wind swept his words away.

Solo had already rescued three people this winter. She was the best dog—gentle and sweet-natured, yet brave. If the lost lady was still out there, Solo could find her. Willie went home to his young family with a grateful heart and renewed determination. Tomorrow was another day.

Jackie was in another land, a beautiful place. She had traveled through some kind of tunnel and seemed to be floating. The terrain around her was beautiful, all blue and white and warm, with trees, flowers, Japanese-style bridges, and the same strong Presence that had been with her since her ordeal on the mountain began. Was she in heaven?

No. She was in the mysterious tunnel again, then back in her body, and back in this horror that wouldn't end. Perhaps this night on the mountain would be her last, but she wasn't alone. Once again, the Presence had reassured her, given her the will to hold on just a while longer. She wouldn't go to sleep tonight. With frozen hands, Jackie dug a snow hole, curled up inside her torn survival bag, and talked to herself. "I sang silly songs, made up stories, thought about the past—just like the night before," she says. "Most of all, I prayed." Perhaps she would meet God soon. She wanted to spend some time thinking about him, time she wished she had shared with him all along.

Morning came, but it brought yet another alarm: snow blindness. "My eyes were barely working," Jackie says, "but I could see that I was surrounded by five-foot walls of snow that the wind had blown around me. There was just a little daylight showing on top." Would they cave in on her before she could escape? Using the last of her strength, Jackie struggled up the frozen walls, watching helplessly as the shreds of her survival bag blew away. She wouldn't live through another night without it. Clambering to her feet, she looked around: still a whiteout, still no sense of direction. What should she do?

Again, there was a light! It shone against the white in a V shape, then vanished. Jackie put her compass position on where the light had been. *Don't go, light.* She started toward it, sliding, staggering, now falling down a steep hill, now tumbling, tumbling. . . .

"Solo! Come back!" Willie and his dog had been searching since dawn and had gotten far ahead of their team. He couldn't blame the dog for being eager, but it was best to stay with the group.

Solo streaked through the snow, her head back, mouth open. She had picked up a scent. Yes! There was someone ahead! Solo ran toward the figure, then darted back to get Willie. From behind them a chorus of barking erupted. Other dogs had caught the scent and were racing forward. "Are you Jackie?" Willie shouted as he ran toward the small, slight figure.

"Yes! Yes, thank God!" The woman had fallen in a heap and was reaching out to hug the dogs as they circled her, yelping in delight. Willie ran to her as members of his search party shouted the news to one another.

It was 9:20 a.m. Jackie Greaves's forty-three-hour ordeal was over.

"She's a remarkably brave and fortunate lady," surgeon Mark Janssens reported to the *Daily Mail* (London) after treating Jackie at Raigmore Hospital. "She required very little treatment; she had slight frostbite on her fingers, but otherwise she was unhurt." No hypothermia, no lasting effects from dehydration or snow blindness—people all over the country were amazed. There was talk of little else for days. Some stopped short of calling it a miracle. But Jackie has no such reluctance.

"God had his hand on me all through this ordeal, from the mysterious light to the railroad barriers that prevented me from falling, even to the awareness that I was not alone," she says today. "And the experience has changed my life." Jackie now spends much of her time visiting the sick, raising money for charity, helping children who need extra attention, and giving back to God for the great gift he gave her: the gift of survival, of course. But most important, the gift of himself.

JANIE'S VISION

Vision is the art of seeing things invisible.

—JONATHAN SWIFT, *THOUGHTS ON VARIOUS SUBJECTS*

It was one of those landmark events, repeated in houses all over Omaha, Nebraska, and around the country too: the first day of school. Janie Murnane's oldest son, Jeff, was about to embark on his great adventure, and Janie was having a little trouble letting go.

It wasn't that her almost-six-year-old wasn't prepared. "We had decided that Jeff was responsible enough to walk to school by himself," Janie explains, "so we had 'practiced' traveling the ten-block route many times. Sometimes Patty Ann, his best friend, came along; and sometimes it was just us. Not only could Jeff lead the way, he usually tugged at me when I slowed down on the hills." The route was long, and there was one busy four-lane intersection—at Saddle Creek and Hamilton Streets—in a commercial area. But Jeff had been drilled, over and over again, on how to cross that street, by waiting for the Walk sign. He was a reliable child, and Janie knew he would be careful.

Now, as Jeff dressed excitedly in his new school clothes, ate a hasty breakfast, and grabbed his schoolbag, Janie was caught up in his joy. She followed Jeff out the front door. "Jeff, slow down!"

Jeff barely turned around. "Bye, Daisy!" he waved to the family dog. "I've got to go to school today!"

Janie caught up to him and took his hand. "You'll be careful, won't you, honey? Especially when you get to Saddle Creek?"

"Uh-huh." Jeff had heard it all before. As Patty Ann came racing out of her house, he pulled away. "See you later, Mom!" he called, running to meet his friend.

Janie watched the children wistfully until they were out of sight.

The day passed uneventfully except for the unusual silence surrounding her. It was later on, toward the time Jeff would be starting home, that Janie began to feel uneasy. Something was wrong, but she couldn't put her finger on it.

Ridiculous, she thought. She was probably nervous because Jeff would have to cross that intersection soon. Hadn't she already told herself a hundred times that this apprehension was normal, something she'd just have to get over?

A chill ran down her spine. No, this was more than anxiety. This nameless dread was growing. But why? Now an all-encompassing sense of danger, fear, even loss rolled over her. Her heart began to pound, and terror engulfed her. Something was going to happen to Jeff if she didn't stop it! Overwhelmed, Janie raced out her front door.

As she ran, the scene in front of her eyes began to change. Although she was on her familiar street, Janie wasn't seeing her street. What she saw—and heard—was a truck, but it wasn't real. It was a vision. Yet the sense of imminent danger, of intense fear, was all around her. "The truck was speeding, bursting through an intersection," Janie recalls. "I could hear children laughing and shouting, the sounds of traffic getting louder, then tires screeching and children screaming."

Nothing like this had ever happened to her before. *God, God.* Her prayer welled up from deep inside her as she gasped for air and kept running toward Saddle Creek and Hamilton. Something she could not understand was about to occur there. *God, give me courage. Help us.*

Janie ran for blocks, speeding by houses. She was getting winded and her legs ached, but fear drove her on. And then the vision was receding, and she was approaching the actual intersection. There were Jeff and Patty Ann! They were crossing the first half of the intersection, walking toward the median, laughing and talking. The Walk sign facing them was on, cars had stopped, everything seemed normal. Yet she was still frantic, the peril around her acute and horrible.

There was a truck, speeding toward the intersection! At the same moment, Jeff and Patty Ann stepped down from the median to cross the second half of the intersection. "Jeff!" Janie screamed, waving her arms as she ran. "Stop! Stop!"

The traffic noise was drowning out her words. The children took another step into the path of the truck. Then Jeff looked up and saw Janie at the curb. "Wait!" She held up her hands. Instantly, he stopped.

Everything in the scene seemed to freeze—except for the truck. Brakes screeching, it swerved widely, just missing the children, and continued on. But they were safe! She had reached the intersection just in time.

"Mommy!" Jeff finished crossing the street, ran to Janie, and threw his arms around her. "Mommy, why are you crying?"

Several years later, Janie still finds it difficult to describe or explain the warning she received, but she is certain it was more than just the product of an overactive imagination. "I've had many premonitions that dealt with Jeff and imminent danger," she says. "Once I felt compelled to run to the park, and I discovered that he had fallen from a slide and broken his arm. Jeff has also overcome some health problems, and God was with us during those trying times too." Janie realized long ago that her children belong to God and are in his hands. Perhaps he is alerting her to dangers because he has more in store for them here on earth and somehow needs her help to protect them. Perhaps she hears the warnings because she is willing to listen.

Whatever the answer, she knows that God is near. "Our family is precious," she says, "and we thank him every day for the love, joy, and laughter we share."

HEAVENLY DREAM

Oh dream how sweet, too sweet, too bitter-sweet,
Whose wakening should have been in Paradise.
—CHRISTINA ROSSETTI, "ECHO"

Not all visions and dreams from God are dramatic. In some, he simply shows his tenderness.

On June 30, 1994, Elizabeth Kingsbury-Puscas's father-in-law, Victor Puscas, died of cancer. He had been a beloved husband and father and a vigorous, respected chief of police in Aurora, Illinois. Elizabeth's husband, Vic, the youngest Puscas child and his dad's namesake, had been a police officer, too, for a while before eventually becoming a lawyer. "I was close to my father-in-law; he was probably my favorite relative on my husband's side of the family, and an all-around fun man, loved by many," Elizabeth says. "We were all there when he died, and we grieved deeply."

Several weeks later, Elizabeth had a strange dream. "I dreamed I got stung by a bee. While it may not seem important to most people, to me it was terrifying, because I'd never been stung before, and I know that our family has bad reactions to stings." Nothing frightening happened in the dream itself. But the next day, as Elizabeth visited with her parents outside on their deck, a bee actually did sting her! "Although I was very frightened, I didn't have as bad a reaction as I had anticipated," she says. "My forearm was swollen just like Popeye's, but ointment was all we really needed to bring down the swelling."

Elizabeth remained a bit leery of bees but almost forgot the incident until a few weeks later, when she had another vivid dream. "In this dream, someone told me that I could visit my father-in-law, and I was so excited and happy, even though I somehow understood that the visit would be a short one."

Then, in the dream, Elizabeth found herself in a grassy, park-like area near a beautiful beach. Mature shade trees lined the edge where the grass and sand met. It was a sunny day, with only a few clouds in the brilliant blue sky, and pleasantly warm.

Victor, her father-in-law, was sitting on a concrete bench. But he was not alone. Next to him was his wife. Elizabeth assumed the couple would appreciate a little time together before she approached the bench, so she stayed to the side, kneeling in the grass and watching the scene. "Dad was telling Mom one of his famous stories— laughing as always," she recalls. "However, he was also playing with a beautiful little girl with long dark hair and straight bangs. She was about four. She'd laugh, get close enough to him for him to tickle her, dash away, then giggle and go back for more." Was she one of the nieces in the family? No. When Elizabeth looked closer, she realized she had never seen this child before. Who was she?

Elizabeth sensed that Victor knew she was there, kneeling in the grass. But without either speaking to the other, the dream abruptly ended. Elizabeth was disappointed that it hadn't lasted longer, but the experience left her with such a feeling of love and consolation that she told her husband about it as soon as he awakened. He was as pleased as Elizabeth was.

That evening, Vic spoke with his mother on the phone. When he hung up, he looked at Elizabeth, puzzled. "Mom finally had a dream about Dad last night."

"Really?" Elizabeth replied. "I'm so glad." Her mother-in-law had been hoping for such an occurrence.

"Elizabeth, it was the same dream as yours. She was sitting on a bench talking with him, you were kneeling in the grass watching them, and he was playing with a little girl she didn't recognize, a girl with long dark hair and straight bangs."

Elizabeth was astonished. She knew that God often spoke to his children through dreams. But what was he saying? Was this meant as a comforting message, that Victor was indeed safely home in heaven? If so, was that the only message?

Apparently, it wasn't. Just a month later, Elizabeth discovered that she was expecting a baby. And on May 31, 1995, her daughter arrived, a baby with straight dark hair and a very familiar face. "Why, this is the child in the dream," Vic's mother told the couple when she saw the infant. Somehow, they were not surprised.

Nor did it seem odd that, just before their daughter's birth, Vic and Elizabeth were cleaning out a closet and came upon a prayer card of St. Michael the archangel tucked away in a Bible that the elder Victor had once used. "Did you put this here?" Vic asked Elizabeth. She had never seen the card before. "Michael is the patron saint of police officers, so we figured Dad had sent the picture, still 'in on things' from heaven," Elizabeth says. "So that's why we named the baby Michaela [Mi-kay-la]." And as their daughter grows, they do their best to tell her about her *mosiu* (mo-shew), "grandfather" in Romanian.

God's ways are not always our ways, and that's why Elizabeth has thought frequently about these unusual episodes. "It seems to me that the dream about the bee sting was God's way of saying, 'Pay attention—something I show you is about to come true.' Perhaps this is why I then took the dream about my father-in-law so seriously. People ask me now if I feel bad about not being able to see my daughter play with my father-in-law, because he was so good with children.

"I tell them I have already seen them together. What a gift."

SOLDIER TO THE RESCUE

Character is what you are in the dark.

—DWIGHT L. MOODY

S teve Campbell still cannot explain why he made a decision that could have had dangerous consequences for him and his family. "You do what you have to do," he says simply.

Steve was a soldier stationed at Fort Bragg, North Carolina. As Thanksgiving approached one year, Steve and his wife discovered that she would have to work on the holiday. Steve decided to take their three children to his parents' house in Radcliff, Kentucky. "During the time we lived at Fort Bragg, I made the trip to my folks' house several times, both day and night," he says. He knew the roads well, and when he and the children started out for Kentucky late on Thanksgiving Eve, he wasn't concerned about the long drive ahead.

On this trip, however, he had taken the family van, which used gas more quickly than their car. As he was passing Lexington, Kentucky, about 2:30 a.m., he was getting low on fuel. "But the last open station I passed in Lexington was on the other side of the highway, with a median between us," he says, "and I didn't want to stop and turn around." He'd be heading onto the Bluegrass Parkway soon, and he knew there would be plenty of stations there. He planned to pull off at the next one he saw.

But to Steve's mounting concern, each station he came to was closed. He realized, too late, that this was probably because he was traveling on a holiday. Nothing would be open today. There was no way he was going to get to his parents' house now; his fuel gauge had been on empty for some time already. It was unusually cold that night, and although the children were snug under the few blankets he'd brought along, what would happen without the heater? He hadn't seen another car in miles, and he knew this stretch of highway had few houses on it. And when the van eventually stopped . . . Well, Steve was a big man and a tough GI, but would he be able to protect his three children if they ran into troublemakers?

Although sputtering, the van continued to travel. Oddly, it had gone almost one hundred miles since Lexington; Steve wouldn't have thought he could get that far. Then his luck finally ran out. The engine died, and the van coasted to a stop on a desolate stretch of road, with no highway lights to show them where they were, and no drivers with cell phones to flag down.

Steve switched off the headlights and opened the door. Might as well see where he was. Maybe a house was nearby.

It was then that he heard it: a woman's voice, calling weakly. "Help. Help me."

It must be his imagination, he thought. Who would be out there at 4:30 in the morning?

"Help." The plea came again. It sounded as if it was coming from somewhere below him.

Thoughts flooded his mind. It could be someone in distress. Or it could be a trap: as soon as he went down the pitch-dark embankment, someone could ambush and rob him. How could he leave the kids alone in the car while he went to investigate? But how could he walk away from someone who might be hurt or even dying?

He made his decision quickly, taking several road flares and setting them up behind the van to protect it. He grabbed a flashlight. "Watch my light," he told his oldest son. "If it goes out, you'll know I've been mugged. Then turn the flares off and lock the van doors." Steve went to the edge of the road and sent the thin beam of light downward. There, in a ditch about twenty feet below, was a crumpled car. "It could barely be seen unless you were standing right over it," he says. "A casual passerby would never have noticed it."

"Help me," the voice cried again. It was coming from the car.

Steve scrambled down the bluff. The car was overturned and coated with ice—it looked, he thought, as if it had been abandoned there for months. But he had heard a voice. He peered inside the wreckage, but no one was there. "Hello?" he called. "Where are you?"

"Here," came the voice. Steve circled the car and found a young woman lying on her side in the frozen mud, her hips and legs pinned under the car. She had been trapped there, she whispered, since she'd lost control of her car and it went over the side of the ditch, about eight hours ago. No one had heard her cries. The temperature was now twenty-five degrees.

Steve took a few moments to reassure her. "I thought I better not try to move her—I might do more harm than good." When he heard the sound of a truck rumbling down the highway, he ran back up the hill and flagged it down with his flashlight. While the trucker called for help on his CB radio, Steve grabbed his jack and the blankets, clambered back down the embankment, lifted the car off the woman with the jack, and kept her as warm as possible. Within thirty minutes she was being loaded into a rescue helicopter. Steve learned later that she had suffered several broken bones but would recover.

One of the officers at the scene saw to it that Steve got some gas, and the Campbells continued on their way. "I honestly didn't think anything more about it," Steve says, "until later that day. My mother thanked God at our Thanksgiving meal for bringing me there at the right time to help that lady." Then Steve started to think about the whole situation. Given the fact that the distance between his parents' house and his was 650 miles, what were the odds that he would run out of gas at the exact spot where a young woman was in desperate need of help? And the fact that the van traveled an unusual distance on empty—was that also part of a heavenly plan?

"Maybe that lady's guardian angel took care of it all," Steve muses. But not without an earthly angel who was asked to accept a mission—and said yes.

DELILAH'S PRAYER

So he commanded the skies above;
the doors of heaven he opened.
God rained manna upon them for food;
bread from heaven he gave them.

—PSALM 78:23–24

Children don't worry about their relationship with God as much as adults do. They accept the fact that they can ask for even the most glorious things, and God can grant them, if he chooses. Brother Leo Keigher, who has worked with the poor all over the world, remembers a little Guatemalan girl named Delilah who once came to him and reported on a wondrous event that had occurred. "Delilah, who was about eight or nine when I knew her, was a very spiritual child," says Brother Leo, "and would never have told me anything but the absolute truth."

Delilah was the oldest of several children whose father had deserted them. The family lived in a small shanty with one bed, a table, and some chairs as their only furniture. Their ingenious mother supported them by making lunches, which she took to nearby factories and sold to the workers there. While she was gone, Delilah or one of the neighbor women would watch the younger children. "After my mother sells all the lunches, she has enough money to buy ingredients for the next day's lunches and the beans for our supper," Delilah had once explained to Brother Leo. The system was working well.

One day as Delilah's mother loaded up her cart to make the trip to town, she called to Delilah. "Today I have left beans simmering for our supper in the fireplace," she told her daughter.

"So early?" Delilah asked.

"I have chores to do in town after I sell the lunches," her mother explained. "I won't be back right away. But you know how to stir the beans so they won't stick to the kettle."

Delilah nodded. She had done it a few times. She was a little afraid of the fire, but she had never let her mother know.

"And you will keep the younger children away from the flames so that no one gets hurt," her mother instructed.

"Yes, Mother," Delilah said, and watched as her mother, pulling the cart, walked up the dusty road toward town. Then Delilah took the children out to play for a while, so they would be less likely to trip and fall into the flames.

As the time passed, Delilah looked into the house several times and began to grow concerned. The flames seemed to be getting higher under the pot, and the beans were bubbling harder and harder. Standing on her tiptoes, Delilah stirred the mixture, but she didn't know how to make it all quiet down, as her mother did. She went to the door uncertainly, watching the younger ones play. What should she do?

Just then, Delilah heard a crack, then another. She whirled around. Oh, no! The pot had cracked—once, then twice, then many times—and beans were running down onto the fire and across the floor. More beans flew across the room, coating the bed and table. The fire sizzled, filling the little room with smoke. It was a mess! But worse, there was nothing left for supper.

Delilah went outside and fell on her knees. "Oh, dear God, what am I going to do? Because of me, our best kettle—and our supper—is ruined. My mother is going to be so angry! Please help me!"

She looked up. There was her mother, hurrying down the path toward them. Delilah grabbed the younger children, brought them into the house, pushed them under the bed, and slid in next to them.

"Why are we under the bed?" her younger sister asked. "Ugh—it's wet in here!"

"Delilah! Where are all of you?" her mother called as she came into the house.

"We're under the bed," Delilah answered, waiting for her mother to scream when she saw the ruined supper all over the room.

"Under the bed? Well, come out! The beans will be ready in just a few minutes now, and you can have your supper."

The beans? What was wrong with her mother? Hadn't she seen the pot, split in pieces from the too-high temperature, and the beans everywhere? Slowly Delilah crawled out from under the bed, her eyes riveted on the fireplace. There was the pot, intact, hanging as it always did from the hook. Inside were the beans, looking as they always did, filling their humble home with a pleasing scent. Dinner was indeed ready.

Delilah never hesitated to ask God for miracles—large or small—after that. She had learned that nothing was too small for him to care about. Even beans.

GUARDIAN ON THE BENCH

*But if these beings guard you, they do so
because they have been summoned by your prayers.*

—ST. AMBROSE, FOURTH CENTURY

Kathy Smith is a wife and mom in East Fallowfield, Pennsylvania, but when she was younger, she lived one summer with a group of girlfriends in Margate City, New Jersey, and worked in Atlantic City. She took public transportation for her daily twenty-minute commute.

Kathy was just getting adjusted to her job when transit workers in Atlantic City declared a strike. She started taking a cab each morning to the boundary of Atlantic City, where she waited for a company shuttle bus to pick up her and other employees.

It was all getting rather complicated, but then a coworker offered to give Kathy a ride. "I pick up several other girls on my way to work—it's no problem," she told Kathy.

"Really? That would be great! Where should we meet?"

"Let's see. I go right by the corner of Atlantic Avenue and White Horse Pike. That's not far from where you live. Just be sure you're there at 6:30."

"I will be," Kathy assured her.

The following day Kathy arrived at the intersection of Atlantic and White Horse a little early so she would not miss her ride. She had never noticed how absolutely deserted and quiet this area was at this hour. "The whole city was like a ghost town," she recalls. "No one was walking anywhere. No traffic, no businesses open."

As Kathy waited, she heard a loud commotion in the distance. A car came speeding down the street, and six or seven teenage boys inside were yelling and swearing out the open windows. The noise echoed through the silence. They seemed drunk; perhaps they were just coming home from a party. As they raced past her, several yelled rude remarks. Kathy ignored them and tried to look inconspicuous. But how could she? "There was no place to hide—the area was wide-open, and no one was out there but me," she says. "If I left, I'd miss my ride, and besides, where would I go? Anyone could grab me at any time." She sat down on a bench that was set several feet back from the curb. Maybe the boys would just go home, she thought.

But they didn't. She heard the muffler and the shrieking tires as they drove around the block again. This time the car slowed in front of her, and two of the youths leaned out, shouting and leering, before they accelerated again. "Oh, God . . ." Kathy began to pray.

Why hadn't some resident been awakened by now and called the police?

When Kathy heard the car coming around the block for the third time, she began to panic. This time it stopped in front of her. "Hey, girl! Get in! Get in!" several of the boys shouted, while others laughed. They were obviously either intoxicated or high on drugs.

What should she do? If she ran away, they could certainly catch up with her. There was still no traffic, no police or other people around. "Dear God, please help me," she whispered.

Unexpectedly, a young man approached from somewhere behind her. "Hi." He smiled. "Have you been waiting long?" He sat down next to Kathy and put his arm behind her on the back of the bench.

"He was dressed like a tourist, wearing a bright flowered Hawaiian shirt and shorts," she says. "He was clean-cut, with the most beautiful eyes I've ever seen." But rather than relax, she was even more frightened. Was he part of the gang in the car that was still idling at the curb? No, she thought; he was obviously sober, and his behavior was quite different.

"Just act like you know me," the young man said quietly.

Kathy was confused. "Who are you?" she whispered.

"Hey, girl, get in the car!" one of the boys shouted again. Now both Kathy and the young man were in trouble, she realized. The thugs in the car could easily overpower them both.

Then, turning once to smile at her, the man got up, walked over to the car, leaned into the front window, and spoke to the group. Kathy could not hear what he was saying, but she kept looking for a police officer to break up the brawl that was sure to follow at any minute. But the next thing she knew, the boys in the car, all strangely subdued, drove away, and the nice young man came back to sit with her on the bench.

"What did you say to them?" Kathy asked, astonished.

Her rescuer just shrugged. "They won't be back. Don't worry," he said.

An awkward silence fell over them. Kathy was aware that something about this scenario was very different, but she couldn't quite figure it out. "Are you on your way to work?" she asked, for want of more interesting conversation.

"You could say that."

"Who do you work for?" Kathy asked.

"I work for the Father," was his answer.

Surely he meant *his* father. "What does your father do?" she inquired.

"Our Father does everything," he said, smiling at her again.

The conversation was making no sense to Kathy. And there, coming down the street, was her ride. She waved for the girls to stop and jumped up from the bench. "Good-bye!" she said to the stranger and bounced into the car.

As they pulled away from the curb, she pointed him out to her coworkers. "See that good-looking man I was talking to? The one in the flowered shirt? He just saved me from a carful of drunks."

"Where?" Everyone looked back.

"The guy sitting on the bench with me when you pulled up. Right there—" Kathy turned around to catch a last glimpse. She should have been able to see him easily, since there were still no people on the street. But he was nowhere in sight. "How did he disappear so quickly?" she wondered aloud.

"Kathy, there was no one sitting on that bench with you when we pulled up," one of the girls pointed out.

"No, you were completely alone," said another. "And I'd certainly notice a handsome man in a Hawaiian shirt!" Everyone laughed.

Were they playing a trick on her, teasing her? No. Kathy had known from the moment the encounter with the young man began that something about it was different—almost holy. One would have to actually go through an experience like that to understand it.

I never said thank you to him for helping me, she thought. But somehow, she's sure he knows.

Part of the Glory

He who has health has hope, and he who has hope has everything.

—Arabian proverb

Some people might consider Kathy Smith's rescue a coincidence. But Father Michael Drury, a priest of the Oratorian community in Monterey, California, doesn't believe in coincidences. Were it not for an experience he had in high school—which some may call a "coincidence" but which he attributes to God's grace—things might have turned out quite differently for him.

Young Michael had just finished his junior year at St. Joseph's High School Seminary in Los Altos, California. That year, in addition to religion, science, history, and English, Michael had decided to learn a less conventional skill: standing on his hands. "I guess it started just as a new gymnastic talent," he recalls. "And I usually couldn't do it alone, that is, I'd have to lean my feet against a wall to get completely upright." But it was fun, and whenever the spirit moved him, Michael would find a wall and stand upside down for a while. Maybe it was a tension release or just a way to keep in shape or do something different—whatever the reason, the teachers had more important details to worry about, and no one in authority took much notice of Michael's peculiar new habit.

During the previous school year, Michael had had a few episodes of strange weakness. The school's doctor had examined him and suspected an ulcer, but tests revealed nothing. The episodes had ceased until Michael returned home for the summer.

"I had agreed to help out at St. Kevin's Parish, with the kids' programs and other things," Father Michael remembers. Work began, but after a couple of weeks, his strange weakness returned. He could hardly carry folding chairs from one place to another anymore. His worried parents alerted their physician.

Perhaps Michael was just fatigued from the last stressful weeks of school, the doctor surmised. "But if he has any headaches or nausea, call me right away," he said. "These are often symptoms of spinal meningitis."

The following day, Michael demonstrated his handstand trick for some of the impressed kids at St. Kevin's. "Almost immediately I became nauseated," he says. His parents took him to the hospital right away.

Michael did not have meningitis. But there was blood in his spinal fluid, so his doctor ordered a battery of tests related to the spine. "Some of them were very painful, but the most painful part, especially for my parents, was the not knowing," he says. Michael's parents and grandmother prayed over him and brought water from the shrine at Lourdes for him to drink. Seminary professors and friends came to visit; priests from the seminary administered the sacrament of anointing of the sick. Michael prayed too. He believed in God, of course—he was planning to become a priest. "But I really wasn't all that spiritual," he says now. "God was not at the center of my life, but on the periphery. I didn't know if he was really a part of all this."

Almost two weeks after Michael entered the hospital, he underwent a myelogram, a procedure in which a dye is injected into the fluid around the spinal cord so doctors can see any abnormalities in the spine. It was the last test the doctors were willing to try, and his problem was finally diagnosed: Michael had a tumor in his spinal column.

The surgeon operated the next day. "It was a long surgery, some eight or nine hours," Father Michael says. "I remember seeing the doctor afterward—he told me that I was going to be okay, that the tumor had been a contained malignancy, and that he had gotten it all."

Some time later, in the doctor's office, Michael asked more about the tumor, and why it had gone undetected for so long. "Young man," the surgeon asked, "this may seem like an odd question, but had you been doing any strenuous activity before you experienced the weakness and nausea?"

"You mean, like sports or something?" Michael was puzzled. All the guys his age played sports.

"Something a bit more specific, maybe something unusual . . ."

Michael pondered. "Well, I stand on my hands a lot. I guess that's pretty strenuous, if you stay up as long as I do."

"That's it," the physician said quietly. "That's what pulled your tumor apart and caused it to bleed. Spending time standing upside down might have saved your life."

Michael's tumor, he explained, was a type that usually doesn't bleed. The tumor had been only a few days away from embedding itself into the spinal cord in such a way that it would have been inoperable. Without seeing blood in the spinal fluid, doctors might have spent several more weeks—critical weeks—trying to find a cause for Michael's strange weakness while the tumor continued to grow, unchecked.

Michael didn't know what to say. Standing on his hands had been just a game, something fun. Did God use such ordinary things to heal us?

"I wish I could say that my faith deepened immediately," Father Michael says. "But after cobalt radiation treatments, life went on pretty much as usual. I recovered, went back to school, then started college. I was just happy to be back on my feet again." From time to time, he did think about the strange coincidence that had kept him alive, but when he was about twenty, he finally discovered the fuller, richer meaning of the experience he had had as a teenager. "The Holy Spirit was released in my life through the charismatic renewal in the Catholic Church. This started me toward a deeper personal relationship with Jesus and an awareness of the meaning of my faith. And when that happened, all my values seemed to reverse. Things that I had once thought so essential—like having the right stereo equipment or a luxury car—seemed secondary, even trivial, when compared to knowing and serving the Lord."

The experience of being saved by standing on his hands also took on a spiritual dimension several years later. "I saw a short animated film called *Up Is Down,*" Michael recalls. "It was about a man who travels through life standing on his head. Of course he sees the world from a completely different viewpoint than anyone else does. The movie's spiritual theme was that *anyone* would, once he or she decided to live by the Beatitudes, the Commandments, God's great love."

Standing on his head. Suddenly, in a burst of wonder, Michael understood that his own experience had been a parable too. "I adopted this symbol and its connection to standing on my hands as a way of looking at my cancer, and at life in general," he says. "When I had the tumor, I was going through life just like most people—seeing things through worldly eyes. And I could have continued doing just that." Instead, Jesus had turned him upside down—in more ways than one. "God's grace is saving my life spiritually, just as those handstands saved my life physically—and now I am really living!"

Few of us can stand on our heads or even our hands. But Father Michael Drury believes that a new faith perspective is available to all of us. "We can choose to be part of the glory," he says. It's really as simple as that.

WITH A LITTLE HELP FROM MOM

Where there is great love, there are always miracles.

—WILLA CATHER

Early fall, overlooking Virginia's Blue Ridge Mountains—could there be a more beautiful season or scene?* Sondra Johnson mused as she and her husband, Larry, drove home from a shopping trip in town. It was always nice for the two of them to get away alone together, even if it was simply to do the mundane chores made necessary by their large family. Sondra glanced at her watch. Fourteen-year-old Robert was probably home by now, waiting for them to take him to football practice. And Elsie, Sondra's Holstein cow, would need to be milked soon. There were always lots of things to do on a farm, but Sondra had learned long ago to leave as much as she could in God's hands. "I was brought up praying,"

she says. "I cannot remember when God was not a major part of my life."

They had less than a mile to go on the curvy back road when, without warning, Larry slammed on the brakes and peered out the windshield. "There's a tree limb blocking the road," he said to Sondra. "But there's something else too."

Cautiously they got out of the car. Larry approached the limb to move it aside, but stopped. "Don't come any closer!" he warned Sondra. "It's smoldering—looks like it's been burning."

Burning? Sondra looked around. There were no flames anywhere. Then, through the leafy shadows obscuring their view, she saw it: a fallen power line just beyond the branch, bouncing and shooting sparks!

"I'll run to the Daneks' house and call the power company," Larry decided. "You stay here and wave away any traffic." They hoped that, since the road was used mainly by local folks, few would be coming along. But if someone did happen to drive or ride a bicycle into the live power line . . . Sondra did what came most naturally to her in any situation. She started to pray.

No one had yet come by when Larry returned. But in his absence, Sondra had remembered something. Robert, waiting at home for his ride, would be wondering where they were. Maybe they could carefully inch around the downed line and leave the scene.

No. She went back to the neighbors' house to make another phone call.

"Other people might get hurt if we leave this spot or drive around it," she explained to Robert. "So we won't be able to pick you up for practice until the power company gets here and turns off the electricity."

Robert groaned. "Mom, I can't be late for practice. The coach will make me run laps afterward."

That was true. And the coach was particularly tough throughout the whole season on boys he thought did not live, eat, and breathe football. Robert's self-esteem was a bit shaky already; she would have willingly carried him on her back to practice if she could to avoid having him singled out for punishment.

But why couldn't Robert come to *them?* She and Larry were less than a mile from their house if Robert took the shortcut through the back field, which he had done hundreds of times. It meant climbing over the five-strand barbed-wire fence separating their property from the Daneks' farm, but he was an expert at that too. "Robert, can I trust you to stay completely away from the road and just run to us through our back field?" she asked. "We can turn around and take you to practice from here."

"Sure, Mom. I'll be careful."

Sondra hung up, filled with misgivings. Had she done the right thing? Walking back to the car, she prayed intensely: *God, please keep Robert and everyone else safe from danger. Surround us with protection.*

No vehicle had yet come down the road, including the electric-company truck. The lethal power line continued to pop and quiver. Eight minutes passed, then ten. Sondra kept eyeing her watch. Robert was a fast runner. He had been ready to leave when she called, and the distance was mostly downhill. What was keeping him? Had he gotten stuck on the barbed wire? *God, I place him in your hands.*

A truck approached. It was the power company. "The electricity is turned off now," the driver announced as he alighted. "Thanks for standing guard."

Sondra barely heard him because, just as she had instructed, there was her son, racing down the field toward her.

Relief flooded her. "Oh, Robert, what took you so long?"

"It was the barbed-wire fence," Robert explained, catching his breath. "I couldn't get over it. It was the strangest thing, Mom—every time I got close enough to grab on and climb it, I felt pushed back. Like something invisible was in front of me so I couldn't touch the fence. Finally, after a few tries, I just rolled under it."

The power-company worker overheard Robert's story, and his face turned pale. He walked over to Robert. "It's a good thing you didn't touch that barbed wire, son," he said. "This live power line was lying right across it. You would have been electrocuted."

Under most circumstances, the laws of the universe (and electricity) work in predictable ways. But since God is the ruler of the world, he can suspend those rules whenever he chooses, to fit his own mysterious plans. Sondra has never doubted that. "But I am still astonished at the things God does," she says today, "not because he can do them, but because he would do them for me."

THE THANKSGIVING ANGEL

When you get into a tight place and everything goes against you, till it seems as though you could not hang on a minute longer, never give up then, for that is just the place and time that the tide will turn.

—HARRIET BEECHER STOWE

For many years, Ivy Olson privately pondered what came to be known as The Miracle, keeping it in a safe place in her heart. "I was afraid that if I shared it, people would say it was just a dream," she said. What other explanation could there be?

But the event was real. Ivy never doubted it because it transformed not only the life she was leading at the time, but her entire future as well. How could a mere illusion have such an effect?

Ivy grew up as the daughter of Seventh-day Adventist missionaries. She spent her teens in a boarding school and went to nursing school in San Diego. Shortly after graduation, she married Michael, also a Seventh-day Adventist. "The sect was very strict," Ivy said. No dancing, no movies, no parties, and so on. The young couple obeyed all the rules, shielding themselves as much as possible from what they regarded as the sinful world around them. But after the birth of their second son, Ivy became restless. Her life was so rigid, so restricted; all she did was work in a doctor's office and then go home. She longed for friends, for new experiences, for laughter and fun. "I tried to explain this to Michael, but he felt other people weren't to be trusted." Michael was furious when she began bringing home library books that presented worldviews different from their own. Yet she lacked the self-confidence to challenge him.

Then one day Ivy passed a movie theater where *The Sound of Music* was playing. She had never seen a movie. But how she longed to, especially one like this! She had heard that the story was inspiring, the music enough to move one to tears. "Can we go?" she asked Michael that evening.

He was horrified. "Absolutely not. You know the rules."

The rules. Ivy couldn't imagine a God so harsh that he would prohibit the pleasure of music. For hadn't he created it?

And so she went alone. "Sitting there in the theater, swept up in the experience, I faced the fact that I no longer believed in the faith of my youth," she said. But what could she do? Leaving would open her up to ostracism by the entire religious community, even by her own parents. Yet staying would involve living a lie.

During the next several months, Ivy tried to share her concern with Michael, but he could not accept her questioning. Finally one day she packed up the boys and some possessions in her car. Perhaps if she got away for a while and thought things over, everything would become clear. Michael followed her to the curb. "If you drive away now," he told her quietly, "don't ever come back."

Ivy looked at him. She wanted nothing more than to save her shaky marriage. But she had tried so hard to make herself into a person whom Michael—and the church—would find acceptable. Obeying the rules and regulations. Hoping to be loved. Obviously, she had failed. With trembling fingers, she turned the key in the ignition, and drove down the street.

"The first several months were extremely difficult," Ivy said. "I found a little apartment near the beach. It had one bedroom, but we had no furniture, so we all slept on the floor together." Michael occasionally sent money and visited the boys, but he didn't contest the divorce. Then he had an accident and was unable to make child-support payments. Ivy's parents, away in the mission field and upset over her decision, offered no help. Everything—rent, food, and clothing—was now Ivy's responsibility.

Ivy's kindly physician-boss was the only one who knew of her situation. Occasionally he "happened" to have an extra piece of furniture that he thought she might use. But her financial struggle was exhausting. "By the time I paid for day care and all the bills, the only thing left to skimp on was food." Yet how could she let her growing boys go hungry? Ivy applied for food stamps, but the clerk told her she earned two dollars above the cut-off point and wasn't eligible. She fled the welfare office, tears streaming down her cheeks.

Worse was her loneliness. She longed for a friend, someone who might provide some interesting conversation or encouragement. How was she going to handle this huge load? Was life ever going to be better? Would there be a time when she wasn't so frightened or weary? Perhaps if she reached out, joined a group, even met some tenants in her building . . . But her lifelong detachment from social situations had left scars. Who, she wondered, would be interested in knowing her, in seeing what a mess she had made of her life?

As Thanksgiving neared that year, life got even harder. No one was going to invite her and the boys for a holiday dinner, Ivy realized, because they had no friends, and no one knew about their situation. On Thanksgiving morning she awakened, aware that she had only three hot dogs and three buns in the refrigerator. There was no money, and payday wasn't until next week.

It was the lowest Ivy had felt. "I put on a brave face—the same face I'd been wearing all this time—packed up the boys and the food, and went to the park. We laughed and played ball, ran barefoot through the grass, and cooked our hot dogs on a grill." But as the trio walked home, one of the boys looked up at Ivy.

"I'm still hungry, Mom," he announced.

"Me too," his brother echoed. "Do we have anything else to eat?"

Ivy's heart sank. They were approaching the stairs to their apartment, and the night suddenly loomed long and discouraging. What was she going to do?

Just then the door to basement apartment number 3 opened, and an elderly lady came out. "Oh, I'm glad I caught you, Ivy," she said, beaming. "I was going to ask you and the children to Thanksgiving dinner, but you were out when I knocked on your door earlier."

"Thanksgiving dinner?" Ivy's older son asked hopefully.

"Turkey and dressing and pumpkin pie." The lady smiled at him.

"Mom! Can we?"

Ivy was staring at the little woman. Who was she? Ivy had never seen her before. True, her days were long and difficult, but shouldn't she recognize a neighbor who lived below her, especially since the woman knew *her* name? Ivy's natural shyness rose. "I—thank you, but—" She began to turn away.

"Oh, Mommy, please can't we have dinner here?" the younger boy begged. The aroma of roasting turkey wafted out the apartment door.

Ivy looked at her sons. How could she say no to them? "I have your favorite potato salad too, honey," the elderly lady said, smiling again at Ivy. Her favorite—it seemed as if it had been years since she had tasted it. The scents and the warmth, but especially the neighbor's friendliness, touched her heart.

"Thank you," Ivy said quietly and followed her eager children into the apartment. It was nicely furnished, with soft welcoming light and a table set beautifully for four. The lady had planned on their company. How odd.

Dinner was ready, and almost in a daze Ivy sat down to the most wonderful meal she had eaten in years, perhaps ever. There was turkey, yes, and stuffing, vegetables, soft rolls, and that special potato salad. But most of all, love. The apartment seemed to be filled with it. It was as if they had dropped into a story, like the ones she often read to the boys, a make-believe scene full of joy and wonder, with their very own grandmother in charge of everything.

"This is marvelous," Ivy said, sighing contentedly as she buttered her third roll. "But I'm surprised I haven't seen you around, Miss . . . ?"

"Oh, I pop in and out." Their hostess beamed again. "How are you and the doctor getting along?"

"Very well," Ivy answered. "I like my job, but I do get lonely sometimes. Well, you live alone—you probably understand what it's like when no one's there." She could hardly believe she was talking this freely about things that had hurt her so deeply for so long.

"Oh, honey," the woman said, leaning closer. "I'm never alone, and neither are you."

"I'm not?" Ivy blinked.

"Of course not. And don't be afraid to ask for help—everyone needs it now and then. More stuffing, boys? No? Then how about dessert?"

They left the basement apartment weighted down with containers of extra food, yet Ivy almost floated up the stairs. She was filled with vigor, a completely different person from the forlorn woman of a few hours ago. She could do it, she knew. She could hold her little family together, no matter how difficult it might be. She was a "honey," someone special, someone worth talking to and caring about, and life held great promise for her. The lady—Ivy hadn't even gotten her name—had somehow shown her all that and more.

The following morning Ivy bounced down the stairs and headed for number 3. She had emptied and washed the plastic containers that had held all those wonderful leftovers, and wanted to return them. She knocked on the door.

No one answered. Ivy knocked again. Strange. It was so early. Where had the lady gone?

What if she was ill? Ivy stood on tiptoe and peeked through the window. What she saw sent tingles down her spine.

The apartment was vacant—no nice furniture, no lamps or rugs or even curtains, nothing but dust looking as if it hadn't been disturbed in months. Stunned, Ivy checked the apartment number. Yes, number 3, the same apartment she and the boys had entered last night. But where was the little table, the pretty napkins? What happened to the dishes and the food—and the wonderful lady?

The apartment manager lived on the same level, just around the corner. Ivy knocked on his door. "Apartment number 3," she said when he came to the door, "do you know the woman who lives there?"

The manager frowned. "Nobody lives there."

"But my children and I had Thanksgiving dinner there yesterday."

He shook his head. "Couldn't have. It's been empty for months."

Impossible. And yet, hadn't there been clues? Her "favorite" potato salad, the questions about her employer—little things she should have noticed, if she had wanted to question them? Ivy headed up the stairs, her mind racing. She had lived through a miracle. For a few hours, she had been graced with a love so intense, so wholesome and unconditional, that it could only have come from one Source. And she would never forget it.

Seven years later, Ivy went to Hawaii to visit a friend, met the pastor of a Lutheran church, fell in love, and married him. There she got involved in a variety of church ministries. In 1989, there was a building boom in Honolulu, and many families in the congregation, unable to pay their skyrocketing rents, suddenly became homeless. "I looked at them, at their bewilderment, their confusion and sense of hopelessness—and I saw myself years ago," Ivy said. She had never told anyone, not even her husband, about her experience that

Thanksgiving Day. But one evening at a church board meeting, one of the members asked, "Before we adjourn, is there any new mission business?"

Ivy put up her hand. "I'd like to tell you all a story," she began.

Ivy went on to found and direct the Angel Network, a self-help group for people in need in the Honolulu area. "We give them practical help," she once explained, "as well as the tools to become self-sufficient. We try to show them that someone is paying attention to them, that they are 'honeys,' even if that's hard to believe right now."

Ivy died of cancer in 2002, but her legacy of love remains.

Angels All around Us

Angels descending bring from above
echoes of mercy, whispers of love.
—Fanny Crosby, hymn writer

One of the most significant societal changes during the past few years is the almost wholesale acceptance of angels and the fact that they are indeed working in our world. Of course angels are often portrayed wrongly in the media, as the spirits of those who have died, for example, or sweet cherubs come to play with us, rather than the army of God, as Scripture has described them. "When you're talking about angels, you're talking about God," points out Martha Williamson, producer of the beloved *Touched by an Angel* television series. "And to most people, God means religion, and folks just don't trust television to treat religion with much respect. As a matter of fact, many letters our second year [on television] were from new converts to the show who had purposely avoided *Touched* the first season, because they were afraid of what Hollywood would do to angels."

But as the involvement of angels on earth continues, a growing number of people are willing to accept their presence, especially at times of catastrophe. During the aftermath of the tragic bombing of the Federal Building in Oklahoma City, many people claimed to see angels hovering over the building or standing in front of it, wings outstretched. Just before US Air Flight 427 went down in September 1994, several children playing soccer in a field insisted that when they looked up to see the plane, they saw angels flying around it.

But an angel's job is not always to "carry us home." Sometimes they are sent to protect us or our loved ones. And sometimes, as Rhonda Christie knows, "you don't even know you need help."

Several summers ago, while living in Mobile, Alabama, Rhonda and her husband, John, carefully tucked their two-year-old daughter, Kellie, into bed each night and then checked her again before they went to sleep. Kellie had developed a habit of dragging a tiny red rocking chair around with her, which both John and Rhonda would often trip over. "No," Rhonda would say to Kellie, laughing, "you can't take the chair to bed with you!" But they would put it as close to Kellie's bed as they could.

One night they followed the usual routine and were awakened hours later by the insistent ringing of the doorbell. John bolted out of bed. "Who could that be?" he muttered, glancing at the clock. It was almost 2:00 a.m.

Rhonda, curious and concerned, followed him to the front door, watching as he flung it open. A young man in cutoff jeans and a white T-shirt stood there, a bike propped up behind him. In his arms was their pajama-clad daughter, Kellie! Incredibly, she was holding her favorite doll and her little red rocking chair.

It couldn't be! Kellie had been sleeping soundly the last time they checked. How had she ended up outside, in the middle of the night, with this stranger? "I think I must have freaked out for a moment," Rhonda recalls. "I couldn't believe what I was seeing."

John was equally shocked. "Where did you get her?" he asked, grabbing his daughter out of the young man's arms.

"I found her walking down Main Street, carrying her doll and that little red rocker," the stranger said calmly.

Rhonda gasped. Main Street was almost two miles from their subdivision, a very busy and dangerous area. Kellie could have been hit by a car, or injured, or . . . Rhonda couldn't bear to think about it. She looked more closely at the young man. He was beautiful, she realized, with blond curly hair and eyes that seemed to look right into her soul.

John wanted more details. He turned for a moment and placed Kellie in Rhonda's arms. But when he turned back to question the young man, he was gone.

"Our street was long and straight, and we should have been able to see him riding down our driveway or on the street on his bike," Rhonda says. "But although we went outside to look, we saw nothing at all." During those few distracted seconds, the stranger had vanished. Rhonda and John spent the rest of the night giving thanks to God for bringing their daughter safely home to them.

It was only later that another question occurred to them. Kellie didn't speak very distinctly at that age and didn't know her address or telephone number. How had the young man known where to bring her?

"This ten- or fifteen-second encounter left its mark on our family," Rhonda says today. "I know that angels are real."

Anthony Coda had joined the navy and was serving on a cargo ship, the *Ariel*. The crew took ammunition to Iceland and Newfoundland and brought troops and supplies back to the States. One beautiful day, the *Ariel* was anchored off Chesapeake Bay, and most of the crew was on leave. It wasn't Anthony's turn to go, and he was restless. He paced back and forth on the empty deck, wishing someone was around to talk to. Finally, he decided to go for a swim. "I went to the well deck and jumped in the ocean," he says. "I'm not a strong swimmer, and I'm slow, but I do like being in the water."

Anthony had intended to stay right next to the ship. But he felt the ocean current giving him a push. Anthony let the current carry him along for ten or fifteen minutes. The ride was exhilarating. But when he finally turned around, his heart sank. He had gone much too far from the ship. "The *Ariel* was the size of a matchbook," he says. "I knew I could never swim back, especially against the tide."

He tried, stroke after stroke. But he was no match for the ocean current, which was going in the opposite direction. Each time he gained some ground—and paused for a moment to rest his now-aching arms and legs—the tide would push him back again. The *Ariel* seemed even farther away.

"Help!" Anthony shouted. But his words blew away in the strong wind. For the first time, he sank underwater; then he pushed himself up, his lungs bursting. Again he shouted: "Help—I'm drowning!" But there was no one to hear him.

Anthony's arms and legs were heavy as logs, and he knew he was going to die. Once again, he dipped under the waves and surfaced again, for what would surely be the last time. He thought of his loved ones, who would never know why this had happened to him. "God," he prayed, tears mingling with the salty water on his face, "please help me." Again he sank under the waves. It was the last thing he remembered . . .

. . . until he woke up on the well deck, lying in a pool of water, soaked and exhausted but apparently unharmed. No one was on deck but Anthony. The ship was as quiet and deserted as it had been before he jumped into the bay.

Did an angel pull him out of the water and deposit him safely back at his post? "I never knew what happened," he says. Except that, with God, nothing is impossible.

Mayre Lou Montessoro had to drop her car off at the auto-repair shop that morning, so her husband, Paul, drove her to work at the tiny jewelry shop. She was enjoying living on Guam and learning all she could about buying and selling gold jewelry from Thailand. "But the store is so vulnerable," she told Paul once again as they rode along. "We're way out in the boonies, and the phone doesn't work there, so of course the burglar alarm doesn't either. I keep feeling like we're going to be robbed at any minute." Mayre Lou's faith had always been strong, and that morning she had prayed for protection for all the store workers, feeling the urge to read Psalm 91. "I had never read it before," she says, "and didn't know what the word *pinions* meant." But it had made her feel a little better, as if God were reassuring her in some way.

Paul tried to console her. "If anyone did try to hold you up, all they'd want would be the jewelry and money," he pointed out. "If you just gave them everything, they wouldn't hurt you."

"I suppose you're right."

When they reached the store, Carol, the owner, was there alone, her husband having been delayed in Hong Kong because of a storm. Mayre Lou began to feel vulnerable again. Just two women in the store today. She and Paul shared their concerns with Carol. "Sometimes I feel like that too," Carol confessed. "But if a robbery ever happens, just hand everything over. I'm sure we'd be safe then."

Paul left, and Carol opened the store. For the first few hours, things were very busy. Then everything quieted down, with just one woman browsing.

Suddenly two men plunged through the front door wearing Halloween masks and waving rifles! Mayre Lou was stunned. For a moment she thought it was someone's idea of a horrible joke, that the guns must be toys.

But when one of the men tossed a paper bag at her and mumbled something that she couldn't understand, she found her voice. "What do you want?" she asked shakily.

The men seemed terribly nervous. Carol reached for the cash box. "Here," she said, shoving it toward them. "Take all the money."

Just then the other man, who had been moving about aimlessly, struck the one female customer on the head with the butt of his rifle. As Mayre Lou watched the woman slip silently to the floor, she realized fully how much danger they were in. "Everything seemed to be in slow motion, as if our brains were rejecting the reality of it all," she says. "It wasn't real. It couldn't be." Things like this didn't happen to ordinary people like her and Carol.

The man who had thrown the bag at Mayre Lou waved his rifle and shouted at her. She couldn't understand him and didn't know how to respond—which seemed to make him even angrier. Suddenly he aimed the rifle at her stomach. Click. Click. Frantically, he pumped the rifle's loading device, ejecting empty shells, but the gun wouldn't fire. *If only I could faint now and wake up when this is all over,* Mayre Lou thought. Surely a bullet would hit her at any moment.

But nothing did. The women and two more customers who had wandered unsuspectingly into the shop were all pushed to the floor. They hid their faces in their hands while the robbers grabbed all the gold necklaces from the cases. The man with the rifle kept it pointed at Mayre Lou's head the entire time but didn't attempt to fire it again. Finally, after stuffing the paper bags with cash, the men took the customers' purses and then ran out the front door without a word to anyone inside. "We expected they would make a noisy exit or warn us to be quiet, but we heard nothing at all," Mayre Lou recalls. "I remember thinking I would lie there all day if I had to, just to be sure they were gone." But after quiet minutes passed and her pounding heart began to return to a normal pace, she lifted her head slightly and realized that she, Carol, and the customers were alone in the store. Slowly, numbly, they began to stand up. "Are you all right?" one asked another.

A gentleman dashed into the store with a description of the getaway car. Carol ran for her car to drive to the police station, because the phone didn't work. The customers were shaky, two of them weeping. The one who had been hit on the head eventually went to the hospital.

One lady pointed to something on the floor in front of the case where Mayre Lou had been standing. It was a .22-caliber bullet casing.

"The realization that he really had tried to shoot me suddenly made my head reel," Mayre Lou says. "That thought still refuses to leave my mind." When she showed the casing to the police, they simply shook their heads. "Lucky lady," they murmured. Why had the gun malfunctioned at that precise moment? Or, if it was in good working order, how could the man—aiming point blank at her—have missed?

The robbers were caught some forty-five minutes later. Since then, Carol has closed the store, and slowly everyone is healing from the frightening ordeal. Mayre Lou finds special significance in the fact that she prayed Psalm 91 that morning: *pinions,* she has discovered, are wing tips. Was her life spared by the invisible wings of angels, circling her in protection? Perhaps she'll never know. But she is grateful for each new day, and each opportunity to learn more about these heavenly guardians.

TOUCHES FROM ABOVE

They that love beyond the world cannot be separated by it. . . .
They live in one another still.

—William Penn

Gifts of love and comfort are probably not limited to angels. For wouldn't our glorious Creator, knowing how much we mourn for those who have gone ahead to heaven, allow them to cross that spiritual boundary occasionally to minister to us?

Swish, thump. Swish, thump. Floriana Hall rocked back and forth on the wooden floor, feeding her newborn granddaughter, Nikki, in the old rocker, and wondered idly how many bottles she had fed to babies during her life. The new parents, Floriana's daughter Joyce and son-in-law Ed, were living with Floriana's family for a while, and everything was going well—except the middle-of-the-night feeding. That one was awfully difficult for Floriana, but she wanted to give Joyce a break once in a while. No wonder God gave babies to younger women.

Swish, thump. The rocker went on with its steady beat. Floriana's thoughts turned to her own mother, who had died suddenly not that long ago. Floriana still remembered how shocked she had been upon hearing the news. Her mother, only fifty-nine years old. Floriana, with five children yet to grow up and have their own families—her mother would miss all that! She couldn't stop weeping about it.

Then one night her mother had come to her in a dream. "Floriana," she said, "I want you to go on with your life. I'm fine and happy."

It was a turning point for Floriana. She stopped mourning after a time and got back to her usual chores and schedules. And now here was this baby, new life filling her home! It was a delightful time, and even though Floriana was enjoying it, she still occasionally found herself thinking about her own mother. How she wished for a small sign, anything to let her know that Mom was watching over them from heaven and knew about Nikki.

Swish, thump. Swish, thump. Little Nikki had fallen asleep, so Floriana carefully carried her into the spare bedroom and put her down. She was a good baby, except sometimes at night when she got on a crying jag. The house wasn't very big, so when Nikki was awake, Floriana and Joyce were too. The men, however, seemed to be able to sleep through anything. They always claimed, the next morning, that they had never heard the baby. The women didn't know whether or not to believe them.

A few days went by. "I think the baby's getting ready to stop that middle-of-the-night feeding," Joyce remarked to Floriana one morning as they prepared breakfast. "She slept until past 4:00 this morning."

No wonder Floriana hadn't heard anything. She hated to admit how grateful she would be when she could have an uninterrupted night of sleep. Even though Joyce usually got up with Nikki, Floriana always awakened too.

The following night Floriana was in a deep sleep when she heard Nikki's little whimper. She squinted at the clock—2:00 a.m. No, Nikki was old enough now to go back to sleep. She didn't actually need this feeding. Babies have to be disciplined too. Floriana told herself all this as she listened to see if Nikki was going to be cooperative. It didn't sound like it.

Well, Joyce had taken the feeding the past few nights. Maybe she should get up. Slowly she swung herself up to a sitting position and reached for her robe.

Swish, thump. Swish, thump. It was the welcome sound of the rocker. How could Joyce have warmed the bottle already? But Floriana wasn't about to argue. Swish, thump. It sounded as if everything was already under control. Gratefully, she snuggled back under the blankets.

The following morning Floriana was cooking breakfast when Joyce came into the kitchen, put her arm around Floriana, and gave her a big hug. "Mom, thanks. You're a doll."

"For what?" Floriana kept scrambling eggs.

"For getting up last night with Nikki so I could sleep. It felt so good."

"What are you talking about?" Floriana turned off the stove as both husbands came into the kitchen. "I didn't get up last night."

"Sure you did. I heard the rocking chair."

"Maybe she just stopped crying and went back to sleep," Floriana suggested. "You know she did that once before." But Floriana had heard the swish-thump of the rocking chair too.

The men were astonished. "I hardly ever hear anything," Ed admitted, "but last night I heard the chair too. It went on and on—I remember wondering if you were going to rock the baby until dawn."

Joyce and Floriana never found an empty bottle, and Nikki didn't end her night feedings for a while after that. But Floriana never again wondered if her mother was aware of what was going on in the family. Mom would be there for all the special events that awaited them. Floriana knew that now for sure.

People of all nationalities and religious faiths have heard of Padre Pio, the Capuchin priest from San Giovanni Rotondo, Italy, who bore the stigmata, the wounds of Christ, for the last fifty years of his life. (During his frequent medical examinations, many doctors confirmed

that the holes were so large that one could almost see through them.)
He died in September 1968, and the Catholic Church canonized him,
making him an official saint of the church, on June 16, 2002. During
St. Pio's life, an aroma of strong perfume often announced his presence, and he could read peoples' souls to determine whether they
were telling the truth. His gifts of prophecy and miraculous cures
were observed by thousands. St. Pio also had the gift of bilocation,
being in two places at the same time. Far from retiring now that he
is home in heaven, St. Pio seems to be using his gifts still for those
on earth who ask for his help.

Doris H., a devout woman who is well-known to the staff of the
Padre Pio Gazette, in Middletown, Connecticut, e-mailed a request
for prayers for a friend of hers named Dorothy. Dorothy had been
fighting cancer, and another tumor had appeared on her arm. Her
physician had told her that if the cancer spread, he would not oper-
ate on her anymore.

"I went to Mass on August 12 and knelt next to Dorothy," Doris
told the staff at the *Gazette.* "Dorothy asked if I would pray that she
would be healed. Of course I said yes." While Doris was kneeling,
she saw a bearded man approach. "When he came closer, there was
a golden light around him, and he smiled at me," she says. She recognized him from the many photos she had seen. It was St. Pio!

Doris was not afraid. Instead, she asked this saintly man if he
would help Dorothy.

"Yes," she heard St. Pio say. "Tell her to pray to Jesus for three days. But she must have faith and show that faith. There is faith, and there is *true* faith. It is the true faith that counts."

Not everyone who prays for a healing, even with true faith, will receive it, St. Pio told Doris. But they all will find peace. Then the priest's image faded. Doris immediately gave his message to Dorothy, who was overjoyed.

On August 15, Dorothy was scheduled for tests. First, she attended early Mass, where Doris caught sight of her kneeling in a pew. "After Mass, I went outside to talk to her, but I was too late—she was already in her car, backing up," Doris says. There was a man sitting next to her in the car. Doris assumed it was Dorothy's husband.

"But when the car backed up, I saw the man's face. He had a beard, and her husband does not." The man turned around, looked directly at Doris, smiled at her, and put up his hand. It was St. Pio!

Doris was flooded with peace, love—and confidence for her friend. "When he said he would be with Dorothy in the hospital, I believed him," Doris explains. But she was shocked to see just how close this wonderful saint was planning to be.

St. Pio was as good as his word. Dorothy came home the very same day. "The doctors were amazed—the cancer has not spread, and they said I'm going to completely recover," she told Doris.

Doris was not surprised. She and Dorothy both thank St. Pio every day for the gifts he has given.

Susan Gibson, a first-grade teacher from Enola, Pennsylvania, had a severe allergic reaction that hospitalized and frightened her. "After that, I started to live my life a bit differently," she says. Susan had once been a member of a church and had sung in the choir. Since her grandmother and aunt still attended that church (and her grandmother kept making pointed remarks about how nice it would be if she came back), Susan decided to go with them one Sunday morning.

"As we walked into the church, which was rather crowded, I saw two friends of mine—Gail and Walt—whom I used to sing with in choir," Susan recalls. "Gail was standing right behind her husband, Walt, leaning over his shoulder, with her hymnal in her hand and her robe on. They both have beautiful voices, and I had always wanted Gail to sing at my wedding." Susan decided that she had to go and give them both a hug. But by the time she worked her way through the crowd, she found only Walt. He was obviously happy to see her after all this time. They chatted briefly, but soon the chimes rang, announcing the beginning of services. Susan went up one aisle and down another back to her pew, sticking her head in the choir loft on her way to wave at Gail and wish her good luck.

But Gail wasn't in the loft. And as the service began and the choir sang the first song, Susan noticed that Gail didn't seem to be anywhere in the choir. Walt was in his usual place, and Gail usually stood right next to him. But there was no sign of her, even though Susan was absolutely positive she had seen her old friend—it had not been someone else. Had Gail suddenly gotten sick and decided to go home?

Susan was holding the church bulletin, and now she flipped through it. On the second page, she noticed the "In memory of" section. Toward the bottom was Gail's name, under the heading "In loving memory of my wife, from Walt."

Susan started to giggle. Gail must be furious at Walt's mistake. Or maybe it was a practical joke. "Gram," she whispered, "look—Walt put Gail's name in the memorials instead of the dedication column."

Susan's grandmother gave her a peculiar look.

"Speaking of Gail, where *is* she?" Susan murmured to her aunt. "I saw her a little earlier, but—"

Susan's aunt pulled a pencil out of her purse and took Susan's bulletin. Down at the bottom, near the memorials, she wrote, "You couldn't have seen her earlier. Gail is dead. She died a few months ago."

Stunned, Susan read the scribble. She couldn't believe it. How could Gail have died without her knowing about it? Why had she not attended the funeral or gotten involved in the mourning somehow?

It was because she had chosen not to be a part of the church community, she knew. She wouldn't let that happen again.

"I eventually told my grandmother and aunt that I had seen Gail that morning in the choir loft," Susan says. "No halo, wings, or bright lights—just Gail. Maybe she was letting me know that she and her music would always be nearby, and that she was happy in her new life. It was a moment I'll never forget."

After giving a talk in a bookstore in Oregon, I asked if anyone in the audience had a story to share. A young man, Joe, told us of a time when he was about ten and was allowed to stay home on Saturday mornings to watch cartoons while his parents and younger sister went grocery shopping.

"My grandparents lived about forty miles away, and on Saturdays, Grandpa often came over about 11:00," Joe recalled. "Sometimes he'd be dressed in his old clothes, which meant that he was going to help my dad with maintenance around the house. But sometimes he'd be wearing something new. I always knew that meant he and I were going out to lunch, just by ourselves."

Joe loved his grandpa and was delighted one Saturday morning to hear the key in the kitchen door. He turned around, and Grandpa was coming in. He was wearing a new green plaid shirt. Yes! It was a lunch day for him and Grandpa. He waved to Grandpa, and Grandpa waved back and blew Joe a kiss, as was his custom. Joe turned back to the television to watch the last of a cartoon.

A minute or two later, he switched off the television and went into the kitchen to ask Grandpa about the details of the day. But the kitchen was empty. Had Grandpa gone downstairs to the basement? Joe scrambled down the stairs, but everything was dark. When he came up, he went outside in time to see his family pulling into the driveway. "Grandpa was here," Joe told his father. "But I don't see him now."

"Well, he has to be somewhere, maybe talking to the neighbors?" Joe's father began to hunt, along with Joe. Grandpa was nowhere to be found.

Puzzled, they came into the kitchen just as the phone rang. Joe's father answered it. Slowly his face turned pale. "I'll be over right away, Mom," he said, then hung up and turned to his family. "That was Grandma. She's home, and she just went into the living room, where Grandpa was reading the paper, and found him . . . dead."

Dead! "But . . ." Joe began.

"He had planned to leave in just a few minutes to drive over here to take you out to lunch, Joe," Dad went on, his eyes filling up. "His heart just stopped. It was a beautiful death, but so sudden for all of us."

"Did Grandma say what he was wearing?" Joe asked.

"Yes, she did. A new green plaid shirt."

Now, some fifteen years later, Joe said that this happening never scared him or made him feel "spooked." "I feel today just as I felt that morning," he said. "I thought it was great of God to let my grandpa stop by on his way to heaven and blow me one last kiss."

MISSISSIPPI MIRACLE

Then the glory of the LORD shall be revealed,
and all mankind shall see it together.

—ISAIAH 40:5

To most of us, rain is just a part of nature, something that brightens our flower gardens or makes driving more difficult. But rain is a biblical symbol as well. As we recall, God once sent a forty-day flood to wipe out the population so he could start the world all over again, because his people had turned against his commandments.

Mary Talken lives on the bluffs that overlook the Mississippi River in Quincy, Illinois. She wasn't thinking of anything as lofty as the biblical flood when, on St. Patrick's Day 1993, she looked out her kitchen window and noticed that it was raining. There were still seven inches of snow on the ground, and farmers were beginning to watch the small rivers and lakes with some concern.

Showers continued almost every day during the remainder of March. There was also a two-foot snowfall in Sioux City, Iowa, and a ten-foot-high ice jam in Minnesota, both of which would have to melt and travel south past Quincy. The townspeople were becoming concerned. "During April, Quincy had hit-or-miss rainfall, with the river depth rising and going down again slightly, but not over seventeen to twenty-one feet," Mary says. "Still, normal depth is around eleven feet, with flood stage about seventeen feet, so people started sandbagging, just to be on the safe side." Hannibal, Missouri, a city south of Quincy on the river, installed a new flood system. Up north in Joliet, Illinois, some residents evacuated their homes. But as one native put it, "If you don't like water, you oughtn't live here."

Experts forecasted a 21-foot crest, definitely manageable. But "the flood that had one chance in five hundred of occurring in any given year—a flood of 31.35 feet," reported the *Quincy Herald-Whig,* was on its way.

The disaster started slowly, ominously. In mid-April, a creek overflowed its banks and reached to the edges of homes. Businesses in several riverfront cities were surrounded by water, and a leak was discovered in one of the levees. "It was muddy but calm," Mary recalls. "People cleaned up the silt from the riverfront parks and assumed the worst was over."

But the rain kept falling, soaking the already saturated ground, making river current flow twice as fast as usual, causing barges to crash into one another, and—once again—raising the river. On

June 30, the first levee broke, flooding an initial eight hundred acres. That night lightning and thunder shook houses, high winds blew down power lines, and six inches of rain poured into basements. The river flowed south at five times its normal speed and broke height records wherever it went.

Fortunately for Mary and most of Quincy's forty-thousand-plus residents, their houses were spared because the city is located high on a rocky hill that follows the winding river for many miles. But some of Mary's friends in low-lying areas were not so fortunate.

By now the flood was national news, and the hearts of many around the country ached for those directly affected by it. Quincyans began around-the-clock sandbagging; the elderly sat in lawn chairs holding bags open while younger people filled them. Others worked the riverbank itself, adding bags to any weak spots they found. Quincy's mayor mobilized inmates from the county jail to help. Locks and dams were closed to let the river flow freely, but this stranded hundreds of boats and caused a traffic nightmare. People flocked to vantage points along the bluff to view the ever-rising water as others continued to evacuate.

"We're going to win this battle," Mary told a group of neighbors when they met one day. "We've been praying, haven't we?" The media had been great too, staying available around the clock, getting messages from people on the levee to those who could bring bug spray, sunscreen, hats, dry socks—whatever was needed.

"It looks hopeful," said one of the women, watching the National Guard patrol while nurses gave tetanus shots. The Salvation Army, the Red Cross, and people from out of town brought food and found lodging for the growing number of evacuees.

But it was still raining.

On July 8, the second levee broke. Floodwaters inundated thousands upon thousands of acres of farmland downriver, and angry waters lapped the roofs of houses. Exhausted residents watched, tears streaming down their cheeks. "We're going down like dominoes," one woman sobbed. By now the Mississippi was at an unbelievable all-time high of thirty-two feet, and homes were being washed away. Would West Quincy and those lower areas still dry be saved?

No. On Friday, July 16, at 8:22 p.m., the West Quincy levee broke, sucking two barges through the opening and rupturing the gas tanks of a flooded service station. The gasoline that spread across the river caused a huge fire. What everyone had most feared had happened: The Quincy bridges were now closed, and there was no way to cross the Mississippi, from St. Louis all the way north to the Quad Cities, for the foreseeable future.

The newly elected mayor of Quincy was both exhausted and confounded. What more could he—or anyone—do? Then gradually an idea began to grow. The people had been praying in their own hearts and churches, but why not have a public prayer service? Obviously, God could help them. He should be acknowledged openly.

Hundreds of residents attended the prayer service, held the following day in the parking lot of city hall. Clergy of various faiths led the group in heartfelt prayer and beautiful hymns of praise. "By acknowledging God as the creator of all things, we asked him to come to our aid and save what was left to be saved," Mary says. Neighbors of all faiths stood side by side, united in a common cause, as perhaps, eons ago, they were meant to be. Everyone went home with a small sense of comfort. Now they really had done everything they could.

The rain did not stop. In fact, a few days later, another storm hit the area. But oddly, the river's depth began to drop, never again reaching thirty-two feet. By the end of August, despite still-continuous showers, the Mississippi had inexplicably dwindled to twenty-three feet, and people were beginning to attack the more than twelve billion dollars in damage that had been caused by the flood of '93.

Did the river stop rising because the people publicly acknowledged God's power and asked him to take control? Or was it just a wonderful coincidence that the situation began to heal after people of many faiths prayed as a community? Were there things more important that God wanted to accomplish in Quincy, things that could happen only if the flood continued for a while? "I think the 'miracle' of the '93 flood was the coming together of thousands of individuals," Mary says. "When times are good, everyone tends to their own lives, so if God had stopped the rain in early June, we probably would have mopped up the mud and moved on in our own little worlds. But perhaps the Lord allowed the rains to continue—or other natural disasters to occur—to bring us to our knees, to pray and to help our neighbors."

Could Mary be right? One person who would probably agree with her is Sister Maurella Schlise, whose story, about bringing cookies to the prison on Christmas Eve, appeared earlier in this book. "Just to let you know," she wrote to me soon after the destructive Midwest flooding that occurred in the spring of 1997, "almost our entire city of Fargo was spared the flood. Praise God! As I wrote to our newspaper editor, I believe it was because we have days and nights of adoration in our Catholic churches here.

"Nothing like this occurs in Grand Forks. Was it just a coincidence that about twelve thousand of the Grand Forks residents had to come and stay with us for a while?"

WHAT NOW, GOD?

There's always an up- and a downside to suffering,
depending on what you do with it.
—Dr. Laura Schlessinger

When we realize how much God loves us and how closely he watches over us, we're apt to assume that nothing really bad will ever happen to God's children, that we are protected in a special way, immune to the problems of life. Nothing could be further from the truth. From biblical characters such as Job to present-day disciples grappling with sickness or difficult decisions, everyone on earth suffers. And while we're going through hardships, we don't always see the whole pattern or understand why. Yet somehow, God can make his glory shine through every circumstance.

Up until September of 1994, for example, Sheila Dawes (her name has been changed) was living what she considered a happy, settled life. She was married and raising a three-year-old daughter. Then her grandmother died after a long illness. "This was my first real loss," Sheila says, "but I had no idea how much of my life was about to change."

About three weeks after Sheila's grandmother's funeral, her mother-in-law died suddenly. "She simply fell asleep on her couch and never woke up," Sheila remembers. It was quite a shock for everyone, especially Sheila's husband, Brad (his name has been changed), the youngest, who took his mother's death extremely hard. "His mother had always been there to catch him when he fell, or to pick up the pieces. I guess he felt he no longer had a safety net." Brad began to suffer from depression, which got worse by the week. Soon he could no longer work, and he completely broke down.

For the next several months, Brad was in and out of mental hospitals, taking a variety of medications, and seeing counselors. Sheila did her best to answer their three-year-old's constant questions—"Where is Daddy? Why is he sick?"—and give Brad the support he needed. She began to work full-time, now that the bills were mounting.

The stress was terrible. Sheila spent plenty of sleepless nights tossing and turning. She had a very sick husband. Was he going to recover, or was he doomed to a lifetime of mental institutions? Where was the money going to come from? How would she raise her child alone? What had she done to deserve this? Where was God? "But each time I began to lose it, for some reason I'd suddenly regain my strength and be able to continue on. We have a wonderful family and great friends who were there throughout this time for both of us." Someone would bring a dinner, or a flower, or a hug. An answer—or an insight—would come. Sheila would sense, somehow, that someone was praying intensely for her, and it would provide her with just the right amount of energy to take another step. She learned to live—and pray—one day at a time, not because she was a hero, she'd explain, but because there really was no alternative.

At the end of January 1995, Sheila's uncle died of cancer. Sheila drove her mother to his house that morning and then went on to work. Her office was about an hour's drive away on a busy expressway. "About fifteen minutes from the office, my van began to make a funny noise. I remember talking out loud to the car, tapping the dashboard as if I could actually persuade it to keep on going. As smoke started pouring from the back, I got scared and pulled off the road."

Immediately a white truck pulled up in front of her. Now Sheila was even more frightened. Not only was she stuck, but there were two strange men coming toward her. There were always stories in their local newspapers about this kind of thing. She started to pray.

As she looked at them, she realized that they were waving at her to get out of the van. "It's on fire!" one shouted.

She had had no idea! As she jumped from the van, she saw that one of the men had a fire extinguisher, and he quickly put out the fire. The other told her that a tow truck would be arriving soon, and they would wait with her until it came. "Despite the fact that the exits on this expressway were few and far between, and I never saw either of the men use a cell phone, a tow truck pulled up about five minutes later," Sheila says. "The two men simply returned to their car and drove off. I never got their names, nor can I remember what they looked like.

"To add to the blessing, the tow-truck driver took me straight to my office, despite the dispatcher telling him his truck was needed back at the shop. These men may not have been spiritual angels, but I do believe God was watching over me during this entire time of trouble. He knew I was close to the breaking point and would need all my energy for the months ahead."

By early April, Brad's release from the hospital was scheduled; he had been a patient this last stay for about four weeks. Sheila was happy about him coming home, but apprehensive too. He was frequently incoherent because his medication was not yet properly regulated, and she worried about whether she could manage everything. Then disaster struck again. "The night before his release, while I was answering the front door, I fell and broke my ankle severely in three places. I was taken to the hospital, had surgery, and was told I would have to stay there a whole week," Sheila explains.

At first she was panic-stricken—what would happen now? "God," she prayed, "why are you allowing all this to happen to me? I feel so abandoned." She had looked forward for so long to Brad's return, and now she would not be there to greet him.

Sheila's parents took her daughter, and Brad's family stepped in, reassuring her that they would look after Brad until she was out of the hospital and more stable on her feet.

After her release from the hospital, Sheila stayed at her mother's house for a while. During the next few weeks, she saw Brad only a few times. Each visit left her in tears, for he seemed no better. "I could not believe I had lost the only man I had ever loved—we met when we were sixteen—and worse, that our child might never get to know what a wonderful father she had!"

Then, like a resurrection, on Good Friday Brad revived. The medications had worked themselves out. Sheila answered the phone at her mother's house to hear Brad's voice, sounding the same as it had before he got sick. "I'm picking you up this afternoon, honey," he told her. "We're going home, and I'm going to take care of you myself. I called my boss, and I'm going back to work on Monday. Make a list of stuff we need for Easter."

Sheila wept again, this time tears of joy. After being so dependent for so long, Brad wanted to get back to his real life and move on. There were times when she had thought this day would never come.

Slowly, as they renewed their life together, Sheila began to look back and see the wisdom of God's plan for her in her most recent apparent catastrophe, the broken ankle. Perhaps she had not been ready to accept full responsibility for Brad when he was not as stable as he needed to be. When she became temporarily incapacitated, other people had to step in and help her.

And yet, why did any of this have to happen? This is the mystery of suffering, which we will not fully understand until we meet God face-to-face. God's children will continue to be called upon to go through difficult times, perhaps in reparation for the sins of others or to help increase one another's faith. We really don't know why.

Yet "while those eight months were the most difficult we have ever experienced, I can say that we are much stronger for having gone through them," says Sheila. "We are all very grateful to be a family again. And I know God was watching over us through those rough times, just as he always does, and it was through his love that we survived."

Wrapped in Protection

Say to those whose hearts are frightened:
Be strong, fear not!
Here is your God,
he comes with vindication;
With divine recompense
he comes to save you.

—Isaiah 35:4

W*hy have I agreed to do this?* Joe Weikel wondered as he stood in the customs line at the border of Communist China, waiting for permission to enter. He was a middle-aged government worker on leave from his job in Washington, DC; why had he put himself in danger with this mission trip?

It was only a matter of minutes, he realized, until he would be caught, pulled out of line, arrested, and sent to jail, possibly for years. For in his innocent-looking backpack, he was carrying fifty small Bibles written in the Chinese language—contraband in this anti-Christian country. When the guard discovered them, anything could happen.

Furtively, Joe looked around for a route of escape. But there was none available. He was in a no-man's-land of urban congestion, consisting mostly of concrete and barbed wire between the bright, modern buildings of the Hong Kong New Territories and the dingy warehouses of Communist Shenzhen. Surrounding him were lines of people waiting to be checked through. To bolt now would signal to everyone that he had something to hide. Perhaps his ten traveling companions, also carrying Bibles in their backpacks, would be arrested too, even though they seemed to have breezed through customs and were waiting for him on the other side.

Inadvertently, Joe had chosen the slowest-moving line. This inspector was zealously checking every piece of luggage before stamping tourists' visas and passports. There was no way the Bibles would go unnoticed. Was Joe's life of freedom coming to an end? *Help me, Lord,* he prayed.

The whole trip had started in such an innocent way. Joe had taken a sabbatical leave from his government job to attend Fuller Theological Seminary, in Pasadena, California, to prepare for a possible career in the ministry. The seminary offered six hours of graduate credit for a five-week mission trip that involved two weeks studying in Hong Kong, two weeks touring mainland China, and a final week in Taiwan. The trip had sounded fascinating.

"In Hong Kong, before we left on our actual trip, we were required to complete a course on the persecution of the Chinese Christian Church," Joe explains. He had learned that during the 1950s missionaries in China were either expelled or jailed, and church services were held "underground," usually in private homes. By the 1960s, government officials had confiscated almost every Bible in the country. Scriptures found their way into China through outside sources, but deliveries were risky because of the strict penalties imposed on anyone caught smuggling. "Right now, hundreds of Bibles are stacked up in this church in Hong Kong where you are preparing for your trip," church officials had explained to Joe and the other missionaries. "We are asking everyone, but especially college students, to smuggle in a few at a time, for persecuted Christians longing for the word of God."

"Isn't it dangerous to do this sort of thing?" Joe had asked, looking for a way out. After all, he was just here to complete requirements for a course, not to become a hero.

"Don't worry. You won't be caught. Guards don't check students with backpacks," church officials had assured him. "They're more interested in jewelry and drugs. Smuggling a few Bibles will be easy, especially for an older seminarian like you."

However, Joe had ended up swinging a backpack onto his shoulders that contained fifty Bibles, more than "a few." The pack weighed seventy pounds when his clothing was added. And he had a history of back problems.

Now, as Joe was standing in the customs line, the guard, only inches away from him, was turning over every item in the suitcase of the man ahead of him. *God, I didn't expect this,* Joe prayed silently, his heart pounding. *Please don't let me go to jail.*

And just as silently came a small whisper: *My grace is sufficient for you.*

Yes. It was. Joe had known that for nine years, ever since he had begun his walk with the Lord. God would never abandon or forsake him. Joe knew that the apostle Paul had gone to jail for his faith, and that the Lord had been there to sustain him. That had happened with countless others as well, down through the centuries. If he ended up in a Chinese jail because he had tried to spread the word of God, then the Lord would be there with him too.

This knowledge, however, didn't still his fear. And the guard was so close now that Joe could smell his breath, fouled by bad teeth. Joe's arms felt so stiff that he could not reach up and remove the heavy backpack. Would the customs agent rip it from his shoulders and throw it to the cracked pavement? Would the Bibles spill out onto the ground for everyone to see? Would he be led away in handcuffs?

The man in front of him had moved through the turnstile toward the waiting train to Guangzhou. Joe stepped forward, his hands out, ready to be grabbed and cuffed by the guard. "Next!" the guard barked in English—but not to Joe. The guard was talking to the man behind Joe, who had not stepped forward. Passing Joe as if he were not even there, the guard beckoned to this next man, his uniformed arm so close to Joe's face that Joe could feel the coarse gray material brush his cheek. "Step forward! Open your suitcases!" the guard yelled to the man behind Joe. What was happening? The guard had looked at Joe with a blank stare, as if he weren't even standing there. As if he were invisible.

Joe started to speak, then closed his mouth. Cautiously, he moved toward the turnstile. One step. Two steps. He could see the anxious faces of his companions waiting just beyond the crude barrier. The train whistled. His friends frantically waved at him. "Hurry!" one called. "We'll miss the train!"

Would there be shots behind him, guards suddenly realizing what was happening and racing toward them? Joe heard nothing but the ancient engine building up steam. Unhindered, Joe strode into Communist China with his fifty Bibles, then sprinted along with his companions to catch the train to Guangzhou.

During the next two weeks, Joe continued to worry as he and the others toured China, seeing ancient temples and other historic sites in Guangzhou and Beijing, even secretly visiting pastors of house churches. His companions had unloaded their contraband the first evening in Guangzhou, but Joe had to lug his Bibles around for a full week, until a pastor came for them in Beijing. Would the police bang on his door one night and arrest him? But nothing happened. (As it turned out, Joe's Bibles had a special destination, and perhaps that's why they needed special protection. They were destined for Inner Mongolia, a vast land hundreds of miles from civilization that had never before received the word of God in the Chinese language.)

Two weeks later, Joe and his companions lined up at the same border station, ready to leave mainland China. Everyone quickly passed through—except Joe. This time, instead of being invisible, he was the center of attention. An armed guard took him to an interrogation room. The mission group leader, Mark, who spoke Chinese, accompanied Joe.

"What is the problem?" Mark asked.

Joe was perspiring. Perhaps his fervent prayer of two weeks ago had not been answered after all. Perhaps he *was* going to jail.

The guard held up Joe's passport and visa. "These are not stamped," he explained. "This means you never officially entered the country. So how can you exit?"

Of course! Joe had gone into Communist China without being seen. His papers had not received the required entry date.

"It must have been an oversight," Mark pointed out.

"We do not make mistakes," an official stated.

What other explanation could there be? Joe and Mark gazed inno-cently at the frowning Chinese guards, who went to the other side of the room to confer. How Joe wished he could become invisible now! *Lord, don't leave me.*

And again, the answer came: *My grace is sufficient.*

Finally one of the guards returned, took Joe's passport, and stamped the current date on it. Then he turned the gears back on the stamp to the date Joe had entered China and stamped the entry box with the proper date. Wearing a sheepish expression, he handed the passport back to Joe. "I guess we are all human," he said. "Have a safe trip home."

When Joe returned to Fuller Seminary and related his story to a group of missionaries, he learned that many other Bible smugglers had been supernaturally protected from danger, perhaps most notably Corrie ten Boom, a Dutch citizen whose family hid Jews in their home during the Holocaust until they could be smuggled out of Holland. Corrie was arrested and sent to the Ravensbrück concentration camp because she would not reveal the location of the hiding place in her home. She brought a little Bible with her, hanging on a string around her neck, even though the penalty for possessing a Bible was a doubling of one's prison sentence. Not only did Corrie pass through the search lines without being noticed or touched, but she also kept the Bible in her cell for months and even used it in clandestine wor-ship services for the other inmates. The guard never saw it.

"God is serious about getting his word to those who need it," Joe Weikel says today. "I didn't fully realize it then, but I do now. His love and mercy never fail."

Like Joe, Richard Tomasello, a lieutenant for the Scranton, Pennsylvania, fire department, has never considered himself a hero. He would tell you that climbing into burning buildings, rescuing people, and sometimes running out of oxygen are things that just go with the job. But he does his share of praying just the same. And like Joe, he believes that God is in charge of "all things seen, and unseen."

On a day in January, Richard's engine company was called to a house engulfed in flames. "There's someone in there," one of the men called to Richard.

"I'm going in!" he responded.

Richard searched the bedrooms first, but there was no one there. "Then I turned to enter the other room, and the full blast of the fire hit me," he recalls. The explosion was so strong that it knocked Richard's helmet off. And there was no water hose here!

He had to get out, immediately. "I broke the windowpanes out around me—I could barely see them through the smoke—and when the glass fell, someone below ran and got a ladder, and also threw a hose up to me." The fire was roaring now, much too strong to be put out with just one stream of water, so Richard kept wetting down the area around him, hoping to keep the approaching flames from burning him. Then his oxygen-tank alarm went off. Only a few moments of air left.

"I backed up to the window and tried to get through it. There was no chance. It was a real small opening, and I was way too big for it." Richard pushed, pulled, squeezed, and wriggled while continuing to wet the flames now licking at his coat, but there was no getting through. He was going to be burned alive, right here, right now—if he didn't die first of smoke inhalation. . . .

No. He wouldn't go so easily. "God, please help," he whispered, then stuck his head through the minuscule opening again. This time he perceived something that had not been there before. He could not see it, but he could feel a barrier surrounding him, keeping him from the dangerous heat and flames. Now he was being lifted; now going right through the window!

Richard came out of the opening headfirst, grabbed the top of the ladder, and made his way down to the street. His fellow firefighters stared at him in astonishment. They had been getting ready to go up and get him, they explained, but via another route. How had he gotten through that tiny window?

When they took down the ladder, they had another surprise: The top few rungs were completely burned. The flames had obviously leaped out the window while Richard was trying to get through it. Richard's white shirt collar, sticking out from under his protective coat, was entirely black too.

Yet although his helmet had fallen off and the flames had been all around him, he had no burns, not even any soot, on his head or face. It was as if he had been enfolded in powerful, protective arms. The situation seemed impossible. And yet it had happened.

Richard's wife, Joanne, had the answer when he related the story to her that night. "It was a miracle," she said simply. And why not?

MYSTERIOUS WAYS

I fled Him, down the nights and down the days;
I fled Him, down the arches of the years . . .
and in the mist of tears
I hid from Him.

—FRANCIS THOMPSON, "THE HOUND OF HEAVEN"

Of course God loves all his children the same. But he reveals himself to us—and calls us to his side—in many different ways.

Craig Turner had always been a "searcher," abandoning his Presbyterian roots in favor of Buddhism and Taoism, studying Nietzsche and Sartre, and finally embracing atheism in his late twenties. In 1991, Craig was working in Washington, DC, and one day ran into two friends, Beth and her husband, Steve. "Craig, would you be interested in going to Europe with us for about a week, to a small village in Yugoslavia?" Beth asked.

The idea appealed to Craig. He'd been to Europe before and always had a good time. "But why Yugoslavia?" he asked. "Especially with the civil war going on there now?"

"Well, people say that Mary, the mother of Jesus, is appearing to villagers there every day, and miracles are happening so that people will believe," Beth explained.

Craig was not at all interested. "I had worked with Beth, and I knew neither Beth nor her husband was strange or fanatical, but I was definitely suspicious of these so-called sightings. I believed that any sort of supernatural or spiritual phenomenon could be explained scientifically and was certainly not indicative of a higher power."

During the next few weeks, Craig tried to talk his friends out of their plans. They had never been to Europe and had paid a large sum for the trip. What if some con artist was taking advantage of them? "Come with us and see for yourself," Beth and Steve pleaded.

"No thanks." Craig laughed. "The next time I go to Europe, I'll visit Spain. But I'll be looking forward to hearing about all the *miracles* you see."

The day after the couple returned from Yugoslavia, Beth called Craig for a lunch date. "How was Medjugorje?" he asked as soon as he saw her.

"Incredible."

"You mean you weren't disappointed?"

"Not at all. Steve actually stared into the sun for twenty minutes."

"But that's impossible," Craig pointed out. "Anyone who did that would burn their corneas."

"Yes." Beth's face seemed to glow. "Except that's one of the miracles that happens there. And we smelled marvelous roses in unexpected places. That's another sign from Mary, that she's near you."

Craig was a bit shaken. He had expected Beth and Steve to return from Medjugorje disillusioned and embarrassed, ready to embrace his belief that there was no God and that the material universe was governed by the laws of physics. Instead, their faith seemed stronger than ever. "Well," he said quietly, "I'm glad you enjoyed it."

Craig tried to forget about Medjugorje and the questions it raised. But one day, unexpectedly, he felt an intense inner urge, perhaps something like a call to holiness. *Pray, pray, pray,* it said, as if a neon sign were flashing those words. Craig ignored it. But the message came back, firm and unyielding, at odd moments. Finally, he decided to acquiesce, just to rid himself of the inner prodding. "Hello," he said, lying on his bed one night. "It's me again."

Craig continued to pray, but he was not living a holy life, and he knew it. As Labor Day 1992 approached, Craig and his girlfriend, Kathleen, decided to go camping in a remote region of Ontario. The first few days were beautiful, as they hiked and canoed around Ragged Lake. But on the morning of the third day, they awakened to the sound of distant thunder.

Light rain gave way to heavy rain, and the thunder and flashes moved closer. "Are we going to get struck by lightning?" Kathleen asked.

Craig laughed. "No chance. There are too many tall trees here." But a moment later, Craig was hit by "the most incredible pain from every side, surging through my body. I knew it was my moment of death, like the electric chair, and I was screaming as loud as Kathleen. A few seconds later, the pain stopped, and everything went black."

Several moments later, the two regained consciousness; they were paralyzed, numb, and terrified. It took at least five minutes for feeling to come back into their bodies, ten minutes for them to feel as if they would indeed live. The inside of the tent smelled smoky because of the burns on their clothes and Craig's singed hair. "When we finally reached a hospital, the doctor didn't believe our story," Craig says. "But for the next week we suffered from odd symptoms."

Because of this lingering shakiness, Kathleen, a Catholic, decided to get some comfort by going to confession. "Do you want to come along?" she asked Craig.

"Sure. I'll drive you," he said.

After Kathleen's confession, the priest spoke with both of them for a while, then went over to his closet and emerged with two platinum medals on chains. "These are Miraculous Medals," he explained. "They commemorate events that took place a long time ago." He blessed the medals and slipped them over Craig's and Kathleen's heads. The meeting was over.

Somehow, the medal felt right to Craig. He got in the habit of slipping it on under his T-shirt in the morning. It certainly couldn't do any harm.

About a week later, Craig began to get strange feelings. Not physical symptoms, which he might still attribute to injuries from the lightning, but "sort of a gnawing or tugging at me inside. Thoughts of Steve and Beth kept popping into my mind. I couldn't get rid of the idea that they were praying for me."

"Kath," he finally said to his girlfriend, "this is strange. I think I have been feeling Steve and Beth praying for me."

"What do you mean?"

Craig explained the images and impressions associated with his experiences, hoping Kathleen could explain it all away with some scientific answer.

"I suppose," she said, "that you *could* be feeling them praying for you."

Was such a thing possible? Probable? Would it matter if anyone prayed for an atheist? *Was* he still an atheist? What kind of atheist prayed—and wore a Miraculous Medal?

A few weeks later, Craig, Steve, and Beth were out shopping together. It would have to be now, Craig decided. When Beth went back to put some parcels in the car, Craig felt a strong inner urge: *Ask him. Ask him.*

"Steve," he said, "have you . . . have you been praying for me?"

Steve looked at Craig matter-of-factly, as if he had been waiting for the question for a long time. "I sure have."

"I knew it!" Craig cried as Beth came back. "I felt it. I really did."

"We believe you," Steve laughed. "We said prayers almost daily for you, your conversion. Sometimes we thought you were a hopeless case."

"Especially when you yelled at us that night in a Pittsburgh bar and told us we were fools for believing in God," Beth added, grinning.

Craig offered a belated apology.

"Craig, do you know what prayer we were saying for you each day?" Beth asked. "The Miraculous Medal novena."

"The Miraculous . . ." Craig yanked the Miraculous Medal and chain out from under his shirt. "Do you realize I was given this by a priest just a few weeks ago—before I had ever heard of it?"

"God works in mysterious ways," Steve said. Who could disagree?

But God wasn't finished sending signs to Craig yet. A few weeks later Craig popped by Beth and Steve's apartment to pick up something. There was a strong scent of roses permeating the entire place. "Wow, where are the flowers?" Craig asked. "I smell roses." The scent was so strong that he felt as if he were standing in a florist's shop.

"I don't smell any roses," Steve said, shrugging. "And Beth doesn't wear rose perfume."

"Steve, the aroma is all over the place. Don't tell me you can't smell it!"

"Nope." The two men looked at each other. "Craig!" Steve said. "You're being visited by the Blessed Virgin Mary!"

Craig remembered the story about Medjugorje. But it was incomprehensible, unbelievable. He didn't want these bizarre things going on in his life. Yet he alone smelled the roses for a half hour, and the fragrance reemerged in his car on the way home. The very next day he made an appointment with the priest who had given him the medal, hoping this man could shed some light on what had been happening.

Yes, that was a lot of dramatic experiences in a short period of time, the priest agreed. "These little gifts from God, called graces, are used to convert people who may be close to conversion but need that extra push," Father explained. They wouldn't happen constantly, because then there would be no need for faith—and people would obey God in order to receive a "prize," rather than because they loved him.

Craig suddenly realized that he did love God. And how gently God had set out this path for him and led him down it. It had started with the interest and prayer of two friends willing to risk rejection by interceding for Craig. It had continued with a near-death experience that had not hurt Craig and Kathleen but had started them thinking about how they should be living their lives. Then a meeting with a priest who had introduced Craig to Christ's mother, and a special sign that she loved Craig as she does all her children, despite his denial of her. Craig knew he was just beginning his education. When he left the priest, he went out and bought a Bible.

Today, Craig is a Catholic, married to Kathleen, and a member of a vibrant prayer group in the Washington, DC, area. His daily journey consists of small steps of faith, steps that he will take until the day he dies. This is the way of conversion.

JUST IN TIME

[God] will not let any of your anguish go to waste.
Instead he will raise you up and use you for his purposes,
making something beautiful out of every tear you shed.

—ANN SPANGLER, *AN ANGEL A DAY*

Charity Smith (her last name has been changed) grew up in a Christian home and went to church every Sunday and Wednesday. "When I was in the ninth grade, my mother decided that God was calling her to attend the North American Baptist Seminary in Sioux Falls, South Dakota," Charity says. The family moved from Iowa to Sioux Falls.

About that time, Charity's health began to fail. Excruciating headaches limited her ability to function as a normal teenager, and she dropped out of most extracurricular activities. Depression plagued her too, but doctors weren't able to get to the root of it all.

"We believe that Satan was involved—I feel he is active in the world today and will do anything in his power to bring down

Christians," Charity says. "The whole idea of spiritual warfare is too far-fetched for many churches or Christians to believe or understand, but I thought maybe Satan was attacking our family because of my mother's new ministry."

As the end of Charity's senior year in high school neared, her headaches and depression worsened. "I seemed to have lost the ability to deal with even the simplest of problems. But like most teenagers, I didn't say much about this to my parents. I don't think they knew how down I was." At the start of one school day, a migraine began to take over. "I lost count of how many pills I took that morning to try to make the pain go away," Charity says. "But finally I walked into my dad's office [he was the school's band director] and begged him to take me home." Charity's dad was somewhat of a stoic where illness was concerned. But he gave in and drove her home.

"I remember standing in the kitchen listening for the sound of his car pulling out of the driveway," Charity says, "and I have a hard time remembering what went on after that." But she knows that she screamed at God. Hadn't she always loved him and been an obedient daughter? Why had he deserted her? What had she done to deserve constant pain, both mental and physical? If he wanted her to die, why didn't he just get it over with?

Charity's mind felt clouded as she walked to the bathroom and reached for a razor. She could do it to herself, finally put an end to the pain. The first few cuts on her arm felt almost good, "like a release." Soon all her suffering would be over. God didn't care about her. Why should she respect his authority?

Then, suddenly, she surfaced from her haze to see both the bathroom sink and her arm covered in blood. And someone was pounding on the front door. Had her father come back? She would have to answer it.

She put her arm behind her, went downstairs, and opened the door. There were two women standing there, both smiling at her. Neither of them introduced themselves. "This world is a hurting place, isn't it, dear?" the first one said.

Charity gulped and nodded.

"But, you know, there is a God who loves you very much," the other chimed in.

"Where is he now?" Charity demanded.

"He's right next to you," the first woman answered. "He will never leave you, even though it might sometimes feel that way. He'll be with you every step of the way. All you have to do during the bad times is just wait and pray."

"You are not to give up so easily," the second admonished.

The first woman handed Charity a brochure. "Thank you," Charity answered automatically. The two women turned around to leave, and Charity shut the door.

She felt amazingly peaceful now, composed and whole, yet baffled. She could see outside through the front-door curtains, but there was no sign of the two women. Why had they come to her house, and how did they seem to know what she was going through? Had they seen her arm? If so, why hadn't they commented on the blood all over her shirt?

Her headache had begun to fade during the encounter with the women, so she went upstairs to put medication on the cuts on her arm. She counted more than thirty-five of them. Had she not taken care of them, or had she kept slashing herself, she surely would be dying by now. Instead, she cleaned up the bathroom, put on a long-sleeved shirt, and went back to school.

"When I came home that day, I quickly ran upstairs to read the pamphlet the women had given me, but it was gone," Charity says. "I looked everywhere for it, with no success. Nor could I remember what the women looked like. But how could I forget, when they had saved my life?" Had the experience been a dream? No, her arm still bore the razor's marks, and she had obviously lost control in the bathroom. "I think God had been listening after all, and he sent two of his angels to save me," she says.

Charity fought depression for another year or so, but she has now conquered the illness and, at age twenty-two, models all over the world. "It still amazes me to see how strong and healthy I have become," she says. "I hope my experience will help others who face depression rise above these depths and remember that there is a Light, and we are never left to fight alone."

Perhaps one of the most tragic happenings to hit any family is the suicide of one of its members. And according to the statistics, the suicide rate continues to climb. Grieving friends and relatives are left with the feeling that they should have been able to predict it or do something to stop it, or that heaven should have intervened. "Where were the angels when my friend killed herself?" more than one person has asked.

There are no easy answers. We know that we have free will, and under most circumstances, God and the angels will not interfere with our choices. Charity was stopped before she could carry out her plan. But many are not. Why? God is the only one who knows, and the only one who should judge the situation.

Those who experience the suicide of a friend or family member, and who do not feel certain that their loved one is in heaven or that they will ever see him or her again, can certainly pray for that person. And maybe the following story will help.

"My experience happened in a dream," says Dennis Higgins, "so it may be easily discounted by those I share it with. But it was unlike any dream I have ever had, before or since."

Dennis's sister Trish, after suffering from depression for many years, committed suicide at the age of twenty-nine. Her family grieved but also worried that Trish had been condemned for all eternity because she had taken her own life.

Shortly after Trish's death, Dennis had an unusual dream. He and his wife were in the backyard of their home, playing with their child. "I went alone to the side of the house, where I saw a little boy I didn't recognize," Dennis recalls. "Right behind him, walking down the street in a pink evening gown and looking very happy, was Trish. 'Where did you come from?' I asked her."

"A wonderful place," Trish told him.

"What is it like there?"

"Would you like to see it?" Trish asked. "This little boy will take us."

In the dream, Dennis agreed. They set off on their journey, and it felt as if they were flying. They approached green hills and trees, all quite beautiful, surrounding a city of lights. Then they entered a room. There were many people there, all dressed formally and getting ready for some kind of celebration. "Where's God?" Dennis asked.

"Oh, no, not here, not yet," Trish explained.

In my Father's house there are many dwelling places. Dennis suddenly comprehended that he was visiting an interim area; the people here had chosen to cut their life plan short and would thus have to wait a while before they could see God and enter into eternal joy. Dennis hugged his sister, found the little boy, and was soon back in front of his house.

Such an explanation is probably not theologically correct. But it gave Dennis enormous consolation. He knows he will understand the whole story someday. And for those who have ever contemplated this solution, Duane Miller, who regained the use of his vocal cords, offers a thought from his book, *Out of the Silence:*

> I've tasted the allure of suicide. It's not an abstraction to me. I've smelled its breath, I've been drawn by its easy release, and through that experience I can say to any of you—those facing physical ailments, relational explosions, financial cataclysm, and vocational rupture—God never stops being God. He has a future for you. Admittedly, for some of you that future may be in heaven, but that's not for you to know, at least not now.
>
> Don't short-circuit his process.

TO SIR, WITH LOVE

Hail Guest! We ask not what thou art;
If Friend, we greet thee, hand and heart;
If Stranger, such no longer be;
If Foe, our love shall conquer thee.

—ARTHUR GUITERMAN, OLD WELSH DOOR VERSE

Bill and Marcia Holton and their three children lived on a wheat ranch in Oregon; Marcia's parents, Verne and Kay, lived next door. The two family homes were at the bottom of Juniper Canyon, with some of the wheat fields on top of the hill behind the houses. "Our neighbors out here are spread apart, and the nearest small town is Helix, ten miles from our ranch," Marcia explains. Sometimes it seemed as if they were the only people on earth. Occasionally Marcia got a little lonely, but she was a woman of faith who prayed regularly that God would watch over her family. So far he had not disappointed her.

One beautiful Sunday afternoon in early spring, Marcia flung open the kitchen door, put boots on the kids so they could run wherever they wanted, and went outside with them. The promise of warmth and sun was all around them; planting had begun. She loved this time of year.

"Mommy, look!" Her six-year-old was pointing to the top of the hill behind the house.

Marcia squinted. There was an animal up there, sitting calmly and looking down at them. It was huge, at least two hundred pounds. A bear? Marcia thought not—its fur was yellow and fluffy. A mountain lion? "Walk real slowly toward the house," she whispered to the children. "Wait there, and don't come back until I tell you."

Then Marcia took a careful step toward the animal. She knew she would have to investigate it before she'd feel safe letting the children play outside again.

Marcia could hardly believe her eyes. It was a dog—the biggest dog she had ever seen, probably part mastiff, part Saint Bernard. Where had he come from? She knew all the dogs in the Helix area, and no one owned one like this. Was he friendly? "Here, boy," she called, putting out a tentative hand.

As if he had been given permission, the dog got up obediently and trotted down the hill, directly to Marcia. He allowed himself to be petted and his ears to be scratched. Once Marcia called the children over, he even let them ride and hug him. "Isn't he nice?" Marcia said. "What shall we name him?"

"I think we should call him Sir," one of the children suggested, "because he deserves respect."

He *did* seem regal. Now all that was needed was Bill's permission to keep him. The family could hardly wait until he got home from plowing.

"Oh, come on—he won't eat much," Marcia teased Bill that night. "Look at him—isn't he cute?"

"*Cute* isn't quite the word I'd use," Bill responded.

"But he seems to love us a lot, Daddy," the five-year-old pointed out, "as if he's always lived here."

"Well . . ." Bill was definitely weakening. Although his in-laws had two blue heelers to help with the cattle they raised, Bill's family didn't own a dog. And what better place for such a big dog than a ranch? "But we'll have to advertise in the lost and found in case he belongs to anyone," Bill said. "And if we have to give him back, I don't want you all to be sad." Everyone agreed.

This cabbie probably didn't know it was his final Sunday on earth, Paul Smith (his name has been changed) mused as he lounged in the backseat, his pistol pointed at the hijacked driver's head. But he wasn't going to leave any witnesses to this last robbery. The clerk in the Walla Walla convenience store hadn't seen his face—he'd locked her in the storage closet before he emptied the cash register. There wasn't much cash, though, and he was going to have to pull another job soon.

But more important was finding a spot where he could hide for a while. He was an escaped convict on the run. Out here in Oregon the little homesteads were so few and far between that he could easily dispose of the residents, then portray himself as a visiting relative or friend if any nosy neighbor happened by. Eventually he'd commandeer another car and driver, as he had this time, and set out again, working his way east. The police would never find him, not if he stayed out of sight for a while.

The cabdriver's hands were shaking. "I-I know you told me not to talk," he said, "but we've gone sixty miles, and my gas gauge is on E. I was already low when you pulled the gun on me, and . . ."

Paul Smith looked out the window. They were passing a wheat field that looked down into a canyon. At the bottom were two houses. He could see no other dwellings around for miles in any direction. Perfect. He could wait up here until dark. "Turn into this field," he told the driver, who obeyed just as the engine began to sputter.

It was a perfect setup, Paul decided as he watched, from his perch on top of the hill, the families move about the two houses. At times, it looked as if the two women and the little kids were alone. He considered strategies. He could go down now, surprising and overpowering the women and children, or he could wait until dark when the men were back, break into one of the houses, and take command of everyone at the same time. But he couldn't afford to make a mistake in judgment, because he had very few bullets left. Ultimately, he had to get far away from here, before the authorities in Washington figured out where he had gone.

It would have to be tonight, when they were asleep and unprepared. He looked back at the terrified cabbie and reached for his gun. If anyone in those houses heard the shot, they would probably assume it was just a hunter bringing down a rabbit.

That night, the Holton family was debating whether Sir should sleep in the house or in the barn. The massive canine, however, settled down easily on the porch across the threshold of the back door, as if he'd always done so. There was no point in trying to move him. Quiet eventually descended on the Holton household. Then, a little after midnight, Sir started to bark. At first it was just a few short yaps, followed by growling, then howling.

"Sir, stop it!" Bill called through the window screen.

Sir obeyed, but a few minutes later the whole process started again.

"What is the matter with that dog?" Bill asked irritably. He got up again and looked out the windows of the porch door. There was no sign of a wild animal. It wasn't all that unusual for a coyote or badger to run through the yard and set off a brief chorus of barking from the dogs next door. But tonight his in-laws' dogs were absolutely quiet.

"Maybe he's homesick," Marcia suggested.

"Wouldn't he be whining?" Bill asked. "This sounds more like aggressiveness. Sir, be quiet!"

Again, Sir obeyed, but only for a moment. He refused to leave the back door to go in search of what was bothering him. But he also barked and growled continuously, as if he was keeping something at bay. It was almost dawn before the adults in the two households all fell asleep. "None of them were very happy with Sir or me that morning," Marcia recalls. "But we all agreed to try him one more night."

That day Marcia and the children played with Sir continuously. Wherever they went on the ranch—into the barn, across the road—he accompanied them. "When we were in the house, Sir would lie in front of the door. Nothing could get him to move—until we came out of the house again."

That night, Sir barked only a few times. Marcia relaxed. He was settling into his new home, and she was delighted about it. She loved him already in a way she had never thought she could.

A few days later, Marcia's dad, Verne, was on his way to town when he passed one of the wheat fields and saw something shining. It looked like a car windshield, but there shouldn't have been any cars there. Verne drove closer until he spotted a taxi with Washington license plates. Something was definitely wrong, and he wasn't about to investigate by himself. He turned around, drove home, and called the state police. "Get your family and your rifle, and lock yourselves in one of the houses. And don't open the door for anyone," he was told. The police were on their way.

Slowly, as the authorities investigated over the next several hours, Marcia, Bill, and their folks absorbed the shocking story. On Sunday an escaped convict who had just robbed a convenience store had forced a cabdriver to take him just past Helix, to their own wheat farm, where the cabdriver had been murdered.

The sheriff took Marcia and Bill up the hill, about one hundred feet from their back porch, and pointed to footprints, several cigarette butts, and a discarded cigarette package. Marcia was shocked. The killer had obviously stood here in the dark, perhaps for several nights, waiting for a chance to come down and . . .

But why hadn't he done so? "I think the only thing that saved all of you was that dog sticking to you like glue," the sheriff pointed out. "If Smith was running low on bullets and had to get past Sir's attack before he could get to you . . . "

"He'd also lose the element of surprise," Bill commented. He had complained about Sir's noisiness. But what would have happened to them if Sir had not kept the criminal away? What would have happened if they had not adopted Sir?

No one knew where Paul Smith had gone. Later, it was discovered that he had flagged down another farmer, taken him hostage, and repeated the scenario across the country. He killed one more person before he was caught in Pittsburgh, about a week after he left the Holton farm. Immediately he was sent back to prison in Washington. Sir stayed with the Holtons for about a year before everyone sensed that it was time for him to move on. Ultimately, he went to live at the fire station in town.

Why was the Holton family spared, but not the unfortunate hostages? It is a mystery, for we know they were loved exactly the same. "In the Bible, it tells us that if we pray, God provides angels for our protection," Marcia says. Perhaps Sir was not really an angel. But that he was sent from heaven, Marcia has no doubt.

OUR GOD REIGNS

I will wash my hands in innocency,
O Lord, and so will I go to thine altar;
That I may shew the voice of thanksgiving:
and tell of all thy wondrous works.

—BOOK OF COMMON PRAYER, PSALM 26:6–7

Barbara Shleman Ryan was working as a nurse at St. Francis Hospital in Evanston, Illinois, several years ago when she began to feel compelled to pray over people. She had an insight that they needed to be not only physically cured but also healed (the two are not always the same). So as she administered medications and bandages, she also prayed. The results were intriguing. The patients she cared for seemed to go home sooner.

Gradually Barbara developed a healing ministry. God seemed to work through her whenever she laid her hands on people. And Barbara began to realize that people were not the only ones who needed healing—in many cases, the earth itself was in need of it. For example, Barbara points out, in some parts of the world where there has been violence, even if the destruction has been over for a long time, very little vegetation grows today. People should be blessing those areas, Barbara believes. "Indians have recognized this need for a long time, receiving prophecies that the Great Spirit wants to cleanse the earth again, this time through fire," she says. "But that sounds so ominous; couldn't the cleansing be the fire of the Holy Spirit instead?"

A few years ago, after she and her family moved to Florida, Barbara's prayer group kept getting a prophecy that God wanted a healing center built in the area. It was to be on the water and accessible to everyone. No one in the prayer group had the slightest clue as to how this could be accomplished. But rather than dismiss it, Barbara thought the idea warranted more intense prayer. "We needed to make a corridor of light to the heavenly kingdom," she says. "So I enlisted two friends, and we began to pray about the idea every Tuesday morning for a few hours. We would, in effect, say, 'Lord, if this idea is from you, please bring it to fruition. If not, please let us know.'"

The three friends met every Tuesday morning for eighteen months. The women occasionally inspected a building or some property, but everything was either too expensive or too far away.

On one particular morning, however, one of the women received what she suspected might be a message from God. He was asking their little group to request forgiveness for what had been done to their Indian brothers and sisters. The women were puzzled, since they knew no Indians and hadn't had any contact with them, but they obeyed. Within minutes, each of them was gripped with a terrible sadness. They wept, overwhelmed with sorrow and repentance.

"It was obvious that some of our ancestors or people from our heritage had, in fact, brutalized some Indians somewhere," says Barbara. "It didn't really have to make sense—we could just feel that God wanted us to make amends for their suffering." So they did.

A day or two later, as one of the women was running errands, she passed a piece of property right on the water. *Now that's just what we need for our healing center,* she thought, and then slammed on her brakes. A Realtor had just approached the front of the land carrying a big For Sale sign. The price was right, and the prayer group ended up buying the land and starting to build their long-awaited healing center.

One day Barbara decided to call on the neighbors who lived near the land and explain what the group was doing. "Since this land was located in the original part of the town, I figured I'd also learn some things about its history."

"Interesting thing about that parcel," the elderly lady in the house next door told Barbara. "It used to be a burial ground for the Indians who died during the seven-year Seminole War. Their tribe was almost decimated—by American soldiers who took their land."

Shocked, Barbara remembered when the prayer group had been inexplicably led to atone for some sort of transgressions against Indians. "Perhaps no one had ever repented for destroying this tribe, especially if it had been done in God's name," she says. So when the group had prayed that morning, they cleansed the land of the sorrow and pain it had borne, just as a group might pray for the healing of a person. Thus restored, the land was then ready for God to renew and bless and use again for something positive.

Many times we haven't realized that the need for healing is extended to all of creation, not just people. Everyone lives where there has been some pain and violence, or perhaps has stayed in a hotel room or an area of the city where grave sins have taken place. A simple blessing or prayer over such a space can cleanse it. And an area needn't be the site of outright sin or evil in order for us to bless it. A story in an Iowa newspaper detailed a group of farmers who gathered to pray over their livestock and seed in hopes of a bountiful year. A growing number of people bless their homes, too, not only asking God to protect the house (and send angels to live there) but declaring it a sacred space, where anger, pain, and suffering will be curbed as much as possible.

This is also why many people feel confident (after asking God's permission) to pray to subdue the weather. "We can speak to things in the environment that aren't going our way," Barbara says, "because we are God's sons and daughters, and he has given us dominion over the earth."

She remembers when she and several others were invited to a Crow Indian reservation outside of Billings, Montana, to give a conference on healing. About a thousand Crow had gathered in the open rodeo grounds with just a light tent covering them, and the bishop had begun to celebrate the Mass. Suddenly a tribal policeman hurried over to where the conference team, including Barbara, was standing.

"We've just heard that a tornado is headed this way," he said. "It's already hurt a lot of people. You've got to stop and let everyone get to safety."

Safety? Barbara looked frantically at the flat plains surrounding the meeting place. Where was safety? *Only in God's arms,* came the answer. Well, Barbara had never asked for a miracle this huge before, but she and the other speakers began to pray quietly in the back of the tent. "God, you are Lord over all the earth. We will take control over this tornado in your name, and stay in the tent. Please protect us and calm the winds as Jesus did."

When the bishop finished his homily, they informed him of the danger. He led the assembly in a prayer to hush the storm, adding, "Let there be nothing but a soft rain all night long."

Time passed. Barbara and the others heard a lot of thunder and felt a bit of wind, but gradually everything died down. By the time Mass had ended, there was nothing more than soft gentle rain, which lasted all night and seemed to symbolize the cleansing action of the Lord.

The next morning, everyone was able to see the destruction: fallen trees on either side of the rodeo grounds. As the *Billings Gazette* reported it, the tornado had raged on a straight path through the land until it reached the rodeo grounds. There it had inexplicably split in half and zoomed around the tent, knocking down trees as it traveled. Then its two strands converged and the tornado continued its rampage.

It's important, however, to pray over nature as God would intend it. For example, Barbara recalls a hurricane heading straight for Miami. Her first thought was to pray that God would divert it. But she soon remembered that Miami had been in a drought for many years. "We needed rain, but not destruction," Barbara says. So the prayer group met all Saturday night—as the hurricane came closer and closer—to pray for protection over their land. About five miles off the coast, the hurricane suddenly stopped. Within hours it had blown itself out and then moved gradually up the east coast of Florida, dumping much-needed rain on the cities there. Only minimal destruction of property resulted.

We don't often use this authority, do we? But, as Barbara says, we can. "We need to be sensitive to the promptings of the Holy Spirit, sometimes in dreams, or through Bible readings when we are being asked to pray, especially for someone or against destruction.

But don't ever forget, we're asking God to make this earth just like it is in heaven. We're getting it ready for the Lord to come back."

Mellissa Miles of Portage, Indiana, certainly wouldn't have believed that praying for a hurricane to change direction was possible. In fact, she didn't know much about God at all. But when her little girl was about two, Mellissa and her husband began to think more about what kind of religious beliefs they would be passing down to their family. "Although we were married in the Nazarene Church, I hadn't attended regularly since I was about fourteen," Mellissa says. "We started attending Sunday services that winter, and then I decided to take a Monday night course titled 'Naza-What?', a three-part series that explained our church's beliefs."

On the second Monday, shortly after a heavy snowfall had ended, the meeting broke up about 10:00 p.m., and Mellissa left soon afterward. Since she lives five or six miles from the church, she sometimes opts to take a gravel back road to avoid some red lights, even though it has a deep ditch on either side. Tonight she hesitated. It would be much safer to drive through the well-lit, well-plowed section of town—but much faster taking the gravel road. She turned onto the back road despite the ditches.

"I had gotten about halfway home when I became engulfed in a very thick fog," Mellissa remembers. "It wrapped the car in a film, and I couldn't see where the gravel road ended and the snow-covered ditch began. In fact, I couldn't see more than a few inches in front of the car."

No streetlights. House lights too far away to be seen through the fog. No way to turn around or look through the rear or side windows. What if she went down a ditch and the car rolled over, pinning her inside?

Mellissa grabbed the steering wheel in a death grip and drove about two miles an hour. She had to get off this road. But she couldn't see a thing!

"Suddenly I remembered our pastor talking that night about how God wanted us to bring all our problems and fears to him. Even the littlest things, even if we didn't think he would do anything about them. So I immediately began to pray: 'Lord, I am so scared. Help me see. Make the fog go away, please . . .'"

Instantly the fog cleared in front of Mellissa's car. Her jaw dropped in astonishment. Had it simply lifted? No, the fog was just as thick along the sides of the car and behind it as it had been before she prayed. No visibility at all. But a narrow clear view in front of her was leading her to safety.

"The little path remained open for me until I turned off that road toward my house," Mellissa says. "And when I looked back, I could not see down the road. The fog was dense again."

Although Mellissa had not specifically taken authority over the fog, she had done precisely what her pastor had suggested: asked God to command the weather for her. And he had.

There are those who believe that the next few years will bring some weather catastrophes—tornadoes, floods, earthquakes, or even other types of disasters—of an intensity and frequency that our country has not previously experienced. The reason usually suggested for this theory is that God is trying to get our attention by lifting his protective hand from our nation, which was founded on religious principles that today are seemingly ignored or even attacked. Whether this will happen or not, only God knows. But it may be helpful to remember that we can pray over nature, ask for protection from the elements, and place ourselves confidently in his hands.

THE OTHER PASSENGER

Heroism is the brilliant triumph of the soul over the flesh . . .
the dazzling and glorious concentration of courage.

—Henri Frédéric Amiel, *Amiel's Journal*

The late and someday-saint Corrie ten Boom, at the age of twelve, told her father that she did not think she could ever be a martyr. "I would be afraid of the pain," she explained. "So I would deny my belief in God—or say anything else they wanted to hear."

"Corrie," her wise father responded, "when you and I go for a trip on the train, when do I buy the tickets?"

Puzzled, Corrie answered, "Why, just before we leave, Papa."

"Exactly. There would be no point in me buying them three months ahead of time, since we wouldn't need them then. Am I right?"

"Yes, Papa."

"And that is the answer to your dilemma too. For if you were ever asked to be a martyr, God would give you the grace to go through with it at the time. You don't have the grace now, because you don't need it now."

So it is with many heroes. They don't start out that way, but somehow the voice of God intercedes, and they find themselves taking risks for him during a crisis that they never would have dreamed of trying otherwise.

For example, Ed and Anne Gove and their nine-year-old son were on their way back to their home in Westford, Massachusetts, from a satisfying vacation in Florida. They had enjoyed the time off but were now beginning to turn their thoughts back to reality. "Ed is a mechanic, and although I've had some nurse's training, I now manage a salon," Anne says. "I was thinking about the people who had taken charge for me—had everything gone all right for them? Ed was probably wondering the same thing."

Then their son pointed at something ahead. "Look!" he shouted. On the shoulder of the road sat a car in flames. What was even more incredible was that no one had stopped to investigate or help. What if someone was in the car? "Dear God," Anne prayed quietly, "we need your help." Ed pulled over behind the car, as she had known he would. Ed was not the kind of man to pass someone in trouble. The two of them tumbled out and ran toward the vehicle. Wildly, Anne waved at cars passing by. A few pulled over, but no one got out to help. The flames were almost covering the car by now.

"Anne!" Ed called. "There's someone in the front seat. But the flames are so thick, I'm afraid the gas tank is going to explode any minute."

Anne abandoned her attempt to enlist a helpful motorist and ran to Ed. Putting her face as close as she could to the driver's side, she shouted, "Is there anyone in there with you?"

There was a pause. Had the driver died already? Then, almost in a sob, came the answer. "Jesus. Jesus is here."

"Oh, Ed," Anne's eyes filled with tears. "We have to try to save her. I just can't stand here and watch her burn to death."

Ed nodded grimly. The victim sounded young. If he and Anne were able to pull her out, and she died anyway, at least her family would know that someone had been there for her. He started to pray as he reached inside, dodging the flames. The woman was apparently lying on the floor in the front of the car, stuck between metal parts and shattered glass. And the fire was so hot! How was he going to do this?

Anne kept praying—Ed could hear her as he wrenched and pried pieces away from the girl, jumping back every few minutes to dodge the flames. "God, let us get her out before the car explodes," Anne implored. During the times when Ed would move aside, Anne would reach in to help pull. At one point, Ed singed his own clothes. Would they have to give up?

No. All of a sudden, the woman was released, and Ed lifted her as gently as he could, up and out and onto the grass as far away from the car as possible. A moment later the car exploded, blowing the trunk lid off. The woman was unconscious and badly injured. But Anne believed that if medical help came soon, she might recover. The woman's eyes flickered, and Anne leaned close to her.

"Was anyone else with you?" she asked again.

"Jesus was there," the woman murmured before lapsing again into unconsciousness.

Jesus would have *had* to be there, Anne thought, sitting back on her heels as she realized the full impact of what had happened. The car was thoroughly in flames. Ed's hands were cut, and he was suffering acutely from smoke inhalation, but he was safe. Somehow they had managed to free a victim from a hot tangle of steel without losing their own lives, when no one else was willing to help.

Eventually, the paramedics arrived, and although they wanted Ed to go to the hospital for treatment, he refused. "After that long drive and now this, I just want to go home," he told Anne.

The young woman lived, despite a difficult recovery. Anne and Ed had the satisfaction of meeting her family, receiving everyone's thanks, and knowing that without their help, the story would have had a much different ending.

"We didn't really think about the 'why' of it too much," Anne says today. "We got involved almost automatically, because we would like to believe that if we ever needed help, some stranger would get involved and help us."

But that sudden surge of grace and energy, they know, could have only come from the other Passenger in the car.

HOME FOR CHRISTMAS

All is calm, all is bright . . .

—"SILENT NIGHT"

Patricia Cleary (her name has been changed), a geologist, was teaching environmental health and safety classes for a small business in Maryland when the Gulf War erupted. Because her husband, Tom (his name has been changed), was on active duty and they had a preschool-age daughter, Patricia changed jobs, taking one that did not require traveling. Cy Miller filled her old position.

"In the beginning, it seemed that things wouldn't work out for Cy," Patricia recalls. "I also stayed on as a part-timer with the original company and was popular with the students. Cy was someone new. He took a lot of heat in the beginning from this close-knit, practical-joking bunch."

But gradually Cy found his place. A proud army veteran, he was gentle and funny too, and the four or five pens always stuck in the placket of his company-issue shirt became an endearing trademark. Patricia grew to love him.

Patricia's little daughter, Catherine, was not immune to Cy's charm either. "One of the exercises we use to train students to decontaminate after a chemical incident is to put them in the 'Man from Mars' suit and pour chocolate syrup on them—the syrup is dark, sticky, and hard to scrub off," Patricia explains. One day when Catherine was at the office with her mother, Cy allowed her to douse several students with syrup. Catherine was ecstatic. "She loved and trusted him instinctively, and they became great friends."

Late that year, however, Patricia noticed that Cy's energy seemed to be lower than normal. Soon the word was out: Cy had cancer. He went through chemotherapy and seemed to snap back, healthier than before. A year later, however, Cy reentered the hospital.

Although by now Patricia hadn't seen Cy in months, she kept in touch with frequent phone calls. "You're going to beat this," she reassured him regularly. "We're all praying for you."

"Keep it up!" Cy would say positively.

On December 22, while driving home from a business trip, Patricia's thoughts turned again to Cy. What kind of a Christmas would he have, stuck in the hospital? She ought to visit him. Impulsively, she pulled onto the Baltimore Beltway and drove straight to the hospital. But when she got to Cy's room, she barely recognized him. "Cy was thin, wasted, not at all the vigorous man I remembered. I knew he was expecting to die, and he wasn't afraid." But Patricia was devastated. All the reports about him from her colleagues had been very hopeful—no one had revealed what was obviously happening. "I realized now that none of us could bear to part with him." And yet when he and Patricia said their good-byes, it was almost as if he knew this life would not go on much longer. "He seemed happy and at peace," she says. "I was the one who was sad."

It was going to be a terrible Christmas, Patricia thought as she drove home. And what was she going to tell six-year-old Catherine? Her daughter knew that "Mr. Cy" was sick. But Patricia hadn't explained much more than that.

Christmas Eve was a busy, bitterly cold day. Patricia tackled her holiday tasks. There were more things to be wrapped, and some holiday cooking remained. She and Tom would have to assemble Catherine's Barbie Dream Boat after their daughter went to bed. Patricia knew she should try to feel happier. But how? God should have a rule against people dying at Christmas, she thought.

Catherine must have been thinking of Cy too. "I'm going to draw some pictures for him," she announced brightly after lunch. "He can hang them around his hospital room. Will you bring them the next time you visit him?"

"Of course," Patricia assured her, wondering if there would even be a next time. Then, at 2:00 p.m., Catherine abruptly stopped coloring. She looked up from her project, frowned slightly at something unseen in the distance, and put the paper aside. "I won't finish this one, Mommy," she said. "Mr. Cy doesn't need it anymore."

"Okay." Patricia, knee-deep in cleaning, barely acknowledged Catherine's comment.

A few moments later, a friend from the office phoned. "Cy just died," he told Patricia. "At two o'clock."

Two o'clock. Patricia looked at her six-year-old. "Mr. Cy doesn't need it anymore," Catherine had said. But how had she known?

Patricia remained calm until Christmas Eve services. "No one had notified the church that Cy had died, so, by mistake, the lector read prayers for his healing." She started to sob quietly in the pew, hoping no one would notice. Cy hadn't been healed. Why? Hadn't they all prayed well or hard enough? Tomorrow should be such a joyful day—but how could it be?

Little Catherine fell asleep easily, and Patricia and Tom assembled the rest of her toys and laid them beneath the tree. The house was frigid due to the zero-degree temperature outside. "Is there any way we can turn the heat up?" Patricia asked Tom as they got ready for bed.

"Afraid not," Tom answered. "That old furnace just can't keep up with this cold."

Patricia couldn't get warm, even under a thick layer of blankets. Maybe her trembling was actually delayed shock and sorrow, she thought. How was she going to get through tomorrow, especially when grief was going to keep her up all night?

But then she realized she *had* fallen asleep, because now she was waking up again. The room seemed bright—was it morning already? Patricia pushed the sleep out of her eyes, sat up, and looked toward the brightness. Cy was sitting on the foot of her bed.

"He looked plump and healthy, just like he always had, before he got sick," she says. "He was wearing his usual company-issue shirt, with four or five pens stuck in the placket, just like always, and there was a warm glow all around him. I remember feeling embarrassed because I was wearing a nightgown, and I didn't think he should see me like that."

"I'm just fine, Patricia," he said. "I know you're upset, but I don't want you to be."

"But Cy, we're all going to miss you so much." In spite of this incredible, unbelievable scene, she felt tears springing to her eyes.

"I understand your sorrow. But please don't let it ruin Catherine's Christmas. Or yours." He was smiling, in the jovial, heart-warming way he always had. "Be happy, Patricia, because there's no need to grieve."

This couldn't be happening. But it was. Patricia reached over to Tom and shook him. "Tom, wake up!" she whispered. "Look!"

Even as Tom roused himself, however, the light faded. Cy was gone. But something of him remained. "Have you noticed," Tom asked, "how warm it is in here all of a sudden?"

Christmas morning was the most joyous of times, for Patricia had been given a gift of great worth. She had been healed of her grief. And now she realized that the prayers she and others had offered for Cy hadn't been wasted after all. Cy had been healed in the best possible way. He was home for Christmas, borne on the wings of angels and the love of his friends.

Tina's Angels

Those truants from home and from heaven,—
They have made me more manly and mild;
And I know now how Jesus could liken
The kingdom of God to a child.
—Charles Monroe Dickinson, "The Children"

Tina Soldan Beers was young when she married in 1985, but old enough to believe that what she was feeling was true love, despite her husband's unstable temper. Raised in a faith-filled Baptist church, Tina felt certain that God loved them, and would help David (his name has been changed) conquer his anger problems and become a loving and responsible husband.

"Our marriage was rocky almost from the beginning," Tina recalls. "I miscarried my first pregnancy, but three months later, I became pregnant again. Then the trouble began in earnest."

David had decided that he did not want to be a father. He became increasingly violent, verbally and physically. He accused Tina of being pregnant by someone else and frequently threatened to kill her. Tina repeatedly called the police, but back then police were often reluctant to get involved in domestic disputes, and they took no action. After baby Lesley was born, David's outbursts increased. Occasionally, he even threatened the infant. Still hoping that God would restore their union, Tina hung on for a while. But when Lesley was two, Tina discovered that David was being unfaithful to her, and it was the last straw. The couple separated.

Tina could not afford a divorce just yet, but she stayed in her Upstate New York community, enrolled in college, received her nursing degree, and went to work at a local hospital. Her mother came to her apartment each day and cared for Lesley. When Tina did file for divorce, David, prompted by his mother, decided to try for custody or extended-visitation rights. "The court proceedings were ugly, lasting about a year," Tina says. "We had to go through mental health evaluations, and although every expert said David was not fit even for visitation rights, he received them anyway."

It was a difficult time, and Tina often wondered where God was. Hadn't she done her best to carry out his will? Tina knew a loving God would not want her to endanger herself or her child in a violent marriage, and she was at peace with her decision to leave. But her spiritual faith had been shaken. How could something so bad happen to a woman who had tried to be so good?

Then, to her relief, David seemed to fade from the scene. She heard that he had been convicted of stealing firearms and had been sent to jail in a nearby community. He served a brief sentence, was released, went to Georgia, and promptly committed another crime. This time, he was sent to prison there. Tina began to relax. Perhaps her former husband would be locked away for several years, and except for the harassments of his mother, who believed Tina was responsible for her son's problems and often called her late at night, life might settle down.

Early in September 1991, after Tina returned home from work one evening, her mother approached her. "Tina," she began, "has Lesley mentioned her 'friends' to you?"

"Friends?" Tina asked. "You mean the kids in her kindergarten class?"

"No. I mean *angel* friends. She's been talking about them a lot this past month."

"Oh, Mom." Tina smiled. "You know how little children are, always making up stories. I wouldn't take that seriously."

Her mother frowned. "I think you should. I think something's going on."

Perplexed, Tina went to Lesley's room, where her daughter was playing contentedly. What did her mother mean? "Tell me about your new friends, Lesley," she asked.

Her daughter looked up, eyes shining. "You mean my angel friends?" she asked. "Mommy, there are lots of them, all around! And they play with me, and sleep near me, and go everywhere with me."

Angels? "Lesley, you shouldn't say things that aren't true."

"But it *is* true." Bewildered, Lesley looked around the room. "Can't you see them? They're children just like me, but they're so pretty!"

A chill ran up Tina's back. She went to see her mother. "I don't know what to think," she admitted. "Lesley's never told lies before. But how would she even know about angels? They haven't taught the little kids anything like that in Sunday school yet."

"Angels are real," Mrs. Soldan pointed out. "They're in many books of the Bible. Why should we assume that she *isn't* seeing them?"

True. But Tina and Lesley were just ordinary people. Why should guardian angels be hovering around *their* house? Tina decided that she wouldn't say anything more about this to her daughter. She would simply watch and wait.

Weeks passed, and the angel activity seemed to increase. According to Lesley, they were everywhere—at the dinner table, in the car . . . Rather than joking, her daughter's attitude was solemn and sincere. Lesley even confided that the angels wished she would behave a little bit better at school! Would she make all this up?

Then one day Tina received a call from a local assistant district attorney she had met during her divorce proceedings. "Did you hear about David?" he asked.

"David?" Tina was instantly alarmed. "What about him?"

"He was released from jail, and he told the prison authorities that he was coming back here to kill you."

"Oh my God!" The nightmare was starting all over again!

"Calm down, Tina. It's all right now. When he didn't show up for his probation hearing, they put out a bulletin on him and caught him. He's back in jail. But it was a close call—he was only a few hours away from here."

She had been in danger, and she hadn't even known it! "When did this happen?" Tina asked the man.

"Last month."

Last month—when the house had apparently been filled with guardian angels. Tina went to find Lesley.

"Lesley?" she asked casually. "What are your angel friends doing now?"

Lesley looked up from her coloring book. "Nothing much," she said. "Most of them are gone."

Of course. There wouldn't be any need for an army of spiritual warriors here now that David was no longer a threat. No. Things like this didn't happen. The timing must have been a coincidence. Tina decided to put the whole episode out of her mind.

Several months passed. Then one evening, Lesley suddenly looked up from the dinner table. "Mommy!" she announced. "My angel friends are back!"

"They are?" Tina had almost forgotten about them.

"Lots and lots." Lesley looked around the room in delight.

What did it mean? Soon Tina had her answer. David had been released from jail again and had been free for about two weeks in Georgia, which corresponded perfectly with the visit of Lesley's "friends." The heavenly messengers didn't stay very long. They drifted away at the exact time David was rearrested and sent back to jail on a new charge.

Tina didn't know what to think. Since no one knew about David's actions in advance, how could Lesley invent stories that corresponded so perfectly with actual events? Surely it was just a fantasy. And yet, there was something so reassuring about it all. Tina had wondered where God was during this whole struggle. Was it possible that he had been right beside her all along?

From that point on, Tina began to watch in earnest. And she was not disappointed. "Whenever David was due to be released from jail, although I would usually not know this until later, the angels would be around in force," she says. David's mother had received his visitation rights after he went to prison, and she initiated many court orders, primarily, Tina believes, to harass her. "Each time one was to arrive in the mail, the angel friends would be there before I received it. Sometimes the house would seem filled with them, and sometimes there were only a few; perhaps the number corresponded with the degree of danger. They became my signal that something that could affect us was about to happen, or was happening somewhere." This gave Tina time to prepare herself and Lesley for whatever was coming.

One might wonder why the angels did not simply remove these troubles, rather than help Tina and Lesley cope with them. Tina originally wondered this too. "As in any turmoil, my faith both flourished and faltered," she says. "I had a few friends who were there for me through it all. And I prayed a lot." Gradually she grew calmer. "Although I never saw the angel friends, I did learn to feel their presence and draw strength from it. And I think both Lesley and I are stronger because of this whole experience."

Lesley Beers is now a teenager and says that her angel friends have not been around for quite a while. Perhaps it is because she no longer sees with the innocent eyes of a young child. But it may also be linked to the fact that her father has been incarcerated continuously for several years, and her grandmother has not had court papers served recently.

"Who knows?" Tina says. "Maybe the angels will be here again someday, hopefully for happier reasons. But I will always be grateful to God for their presence and their protection." They came, she says, when she needed hope most.

AND A LITTLE CHILD
SHALL LEAD THEM

Trailing clouds of glory do we come
From God, who is our home:
Heaven lies about us in our infancy!
—WILLIAM WORDSWORTH,
"ODE ON INTIMATIONS OF IMMORTALITY FROM
RECOLLECTIONS OF EARLY CHILDHOOD"

As we've seen, children do seem to have a special spiritual aware-ness, at least during their early years. Carol Biddle, of Windsor, Ontario, has a daughter who manifested many typical behaviors. "When Meaghan was a baby, I learned not to go to her right away when she awakened, because she liked to spend time alone in her crib, and even seemed somewhat annoyed when I 'interrupted' her." Meaghan would talk for long periods of time in "baby babble," but with pauses, as if she was listening to responses from someone else.

"As she grew, she had several invisible friends, all with different names and personalities. They would go with her everywhere, even being 'buckled up' when we got into the car. Meaghan also had an odd way of guessing who was on the phone or at the door before I answered it. When she was two, she told me I had a baby in my tummy, and I did, although I didn't yet know it."

When Meaghan was about four, she announced, "When I turn five, Ghostie [her main imaginary friend] and all my other friends will disappear. Invisible people don't live past five years old."

They did indeed disappear after Meaghan's fifth birthday, Carol says. "And we have never heard of them again. She also quit telling me who was at the door or on the phone. It was a sad time for my husband and me when Ghostie, Katrina, and the other friends left us."

Children also seem to interact frequently with those who have died. Since they are too young to fear this transition, perhaps it seems quite normal to them. Jessica Morello, now a teenager, was about seven when her beloved grandmother died. "I was grieving as I fell asleep one night," she says. How could she bear this loss? Had Gram truly gone away forever? "Then, in the middle of the night, I awakened, and there was Gram sitting at the foot of my bed, her arms open to comfort me."

The two played some games and had a party with their favorite menu—cherry Kool-Aid and Gram's special white whipped-cream cake. "Gram told me that she would help me through the rough times to come, and no matter what, she would always be with me," Jessica says. The little girl fell blissfully asleep.

It would have been a simple matter to dismiss Jessica's experience as a dream. Except that, the next morning, Jessica awakened to her father's concerned face over her. "Jessica, how did all these red stains get on your pillowcase?" he demanded. "And you've got white icing on your cheeks!"

Mary Ann, a friend of mine, lost her sister to cancer. The young woman left an eighteen-month-old son. One day when Mary Ann and her nephew were shopping in the produce section of a large market, the little boy suddenly straightened up, pointed, and with face aglow turned to his aunt. "Look, Aunt Mary Ann!" he cried joyfully. "There's Mommy!"

Mary Ann turned to look in the direction her nephew was pointing. There was absolutely no one there, not even a shopper. And yet the child remained elated throughout the rest of the day. "I saw Mommy!" he told anyone who would listen.

Some experts believe that, during their early years, children do indeed have visions of angels or loved ones in heaven, and that such episodes wane as the child moves into more worldly activities. Yet "perhaps we [all] carry this memory unaware throughout our life," observed the great Christian mystic Agnes Sanford. "Why else the deep nostalgia, the wave of homesickness for heaven that sweeps over us at unexpected moments?"

Another phenomenon involves prenatal awareness. Interviewed on ABC's *Prime Time Live* in October 1997, the mother of the famous Dilley sextuplets commented that all through her pregnancy, everyone was anticipating five babies. They were astonished when a sixth—Adrian—emerged; he had been hidden from the ultrasound camera behind Mrs. Dilley's spleen. Yet as her brood learned to speak, everyone told her that they had seen Adrian "when we were in your tummy."

And in another instance, a reader, seven months pregnant, was involved in a frightening automobile accident. She was taken to the hospital, treated, and dismissed, with no damage apparently suffered by her unborn baby. But despite the fact that the mother never mentioned this accident to her daughter, the baby would begin to cry whenever they passed the site of the collision. And as she got older, she told her mother, "This place scares me. I didn't like that crash."

Since children do seem to be "heaven connected" in special ways, it makes sense to develop their natural spirituality early, believes Helen Beason, who has been an educator for more than twenty-five years, as well as a children's pastor. Several years ago, Helen came across a passage from Deuteronomy that had a profound effect on her. "Take these words of mine into your heart and soul," the lines read. "Teach them to your children, speaking of them at home and abroad, whether you are busy or at rest." Helen thought about the typical children's church programs, not only in communities she had been a part of, but also across the country. Rarely, if ever, were children being recognized as and trained to be prayer warriors; few of them were exhibiting changed lives as a result of religious instruction. Because educators generally assumed that youngsters would have neither the ability to pray and worship on behalf of others nor the interest, they limited their teaching to Bible stories or, as Helen puts it, "the same old thing in new packages. But there just had to be more."

Helen believed that a fertile spiritual field was being ignored. "It has been common practice to place only adults in areas of prayer, service, and ministry," she says. "Yet the Scriptures give us plenty of examples of children and teens being used by God in mighty ways. Youngsters raised within a strong spiritual family today are waiting, no, *straining* to become effective members of the Body of Christ, not to sit on the sidelines until they are older." After all, the Holy Spirit—if allowed to do so—can teach *all* ages and compete with any of the worldly enticements our children face.

In early 1992, when Helen was children's pastor at the Living Word Church in New Wilmington, Pennsylvania, she decided to test some of her theories. She started by encouraging expectant parents within the church community to read the Bible, sing hymns, and pray aloud so their unborn children could hear, and possibly respond (just as the tiny John the Baptist leapt in his mother's womb when Mary approached and spoke). "The parents were excited to try something new for their unborn infants," Helen says.

When tots came to the nurseries on Sunday mornings, "we put away the babysitting mentality," Helen says. Instead, workers prayed blessings over each child, recited Scripture, and played worship music. Toddlers were trained to lay hands on one another and pray for one another. Things did not always go smoothly, but the adults began to notice a calmer, more receptive attitude among the toddlers. One twenty-month-old actually implored his mother at home, again and again, to "Pray—Rachel!" Although his mother wasn't sure just what was going on, she prayed with him each time he asked. Later, the adults discovered that Helen's teenage daughter Rachel, serving in a mission in France, had been hospitalized. No one could have known she was in distress, except the Holy Spirit—who passed on the need for intercessory prayer to a child still in diapers!

Noting the success with the church's toddlers, Helen wondered about the older children, especially those aged four through twelve. She felt certain God was asking her to form and train them too. But how? And would any be interested? On July 19, 1992, she put an announcement into the church bulletin about a new gathering: SWAT (Spiritual Warfare Advanced Training). "If your child desires to become a mighty warrior for God, bring him to the trailer room thirty minutes before the main service next week," the ad said.

Helen assumed that a few children would be dragged to the meeting just because their parents wanted to support her. She was not, however, prepared for twenty-five young recruits, most so enthusiastic that they had persuaded their parents to bring them early. But as the group began to pray, spontaneously and without a specific format, Helen could feel the strong presence of the Holy Spirit. Several children suddenly received the gift of tongues, a new prayer language. Others told Helen of their deep-seated longing to participate more fully in the kingdom.

Helen was overwhelmed. During the next several months, as membership climbed to sixty-five children, she and the other leaders taught their small charges how to pray over one another or for those far away (some children would actually hold a globe and weep, interceding for unknown youngsters in foreign lands), to stay focused and listen for God's directions, to pray in tongues, and to read Scripture with thoughtfulness and faith. The children became comfortable breaking into small groups of four or five to pray over someone as a team. Gradually they moved into pre-service prayer, participating with the adults before the main church service.

A year later, Helen added a weekday night to SWAT's schedule and expanded the age range to four through eighteen. "Even now we do not separate by age but work with the whole group," she says. "It is not uncommon for even the youngest to participate with a prayer, a vision, or a prophetic word." As the children get older, they are appointed junior staff members or are sent out with the adult staff to visit other kids "and help them catch the flame of excitement in serving the Lord in active ministry."

While Helen was busy training children in Pennsylvania, Sue Young of Bradenton, Florida, was receiving a similar message. A youth pastor working mainly with teenagers, she began to get one of those inner urges that so often is a prod from God. "I sensed that he wanted me to work with younger children in some capacity," she says. "But I liked teens and was trained for this age group. I was afraid if I prayed about it, I might actually get the answer I *didn't* want. So I ignored the whole thing."

Sue had recently moved to Bradenton's Christian Retreat Center, which is a nondenominational international training center for conferences, with a church, mission programs, and even housing for people who wish to live more closely within a Christian community. She was an administrative secretary there at the moment but still worked with teens whenever possible.

"One night I was asked to substitute for the teacher who taught fifth- and sixth-grade girls," Sue recalls. "I didn't want to get involved with that age group but reluctantly agreed to help out." At the beginning of the class, everyone started to pray. And then Sue watched in amazement as the Holy Spirit seemed to sweep through the room—just as the Bible describes Pentecost. Some of the girls began to weep. "God wants us to lay hands on the sick," one said. "We all know he does. He wants us to use the gifts he's given us *now,* and not wait till we're all grown up." Several of the girls fell to the ground, while others began to pray in tongues. Sue sat openmouthed. She had been at meetings like this with adults and certainly knew of the power of the Holy Spirit. But she had never experienced anything like this with children.

The meeting ended prayerfully, but Sue wasn't quite sure what to think. She was convinced of the girls' sincerity, but she wasn't their teacher and had no authority to establish a format like this. "And I didn't want to admit that God probably *was* calling me to minister to younger children," she says.

But the following night, Sue was asked to sub again—this time, for the fifth- and sixth-grade boys' class. And again, the same mighty manifestations occurred. The boys were as powerful and prayerful as the girls had been. What was going on?

By the following week, when the third- and fourth-grade teacher resigned and Sue was "coincidentally" asked to take her place, Sue saw the heavenly writing on the wall. God was doing something in this community, and she would have to follow his lead.

Sometime later, the founder of Christian Retreat returned from a trip to Pennsylvania, and he called his staff together. In astonishment, Sue listened as he told the group about a woman he had met—Pastor Helen Beason—and the amazing things happening with the children in her church. "Wow!" Sue exploded. "I have to meet this woman!"

Sue called Helen immediately. Not only was Helen planning a vacation—to Florida!—but she was leaving that very day. Sue had phoned her just in time, and ultimately the two women met. Eventually, Sue and her staff brought some of the children to Helen's training camp. "God really inspired them," Helen recalls, "and when they went back to Florida, they took the fire with them." With Helen's help, Sue formed another branch of SWAT and now has several hundred active members. "On Saturday mornings, we go to the housing projects and the migrant workers' camps, and our children—sometimes over a hundred of them—conduct a Sunday school, complete with praise and worship, and pray over the project children for healing and help," Sue says. "It's amazing to see it. There seems no limit to what God is allowing the kids to do today."

Across the country in River Forest, Illinois, in April 1996, Tim Holmes, a young husband and father, was facing devastating news. He had been diagnosed with non-Hodgkin's lymphoma and was presently receiving chemotherapy treatments. "A great deal of love was being poured out on us at this time," Tim recalls. "My wife, Jan, was a spiritual and emotional rock, as were my in-laws, Jackie and Jerry Spierenburg, who had left their home in Bradenton, Florida, to move into our house and take care of whatever needed doing." Friends rallied around, and people from St. Luke's Parish as well as the First Presbyterian Church, where Tim's children attended Sunday school, offered support and prayers. Tim's business partner took over running the office. But when the chemotherapy treatments ended in September, physicians found a new tumor in Tim's chest. There was nothing to be done now except an autologous bone-marrow transplant, followed by radiation and an experimental therapy: Interleukin-2.

"The whole process would take four months, starting at the end of October," Tim says. "It would be mentally and physically challenging. But we had no choice but to schedule it, and once again, people came to our aid, even offering their own bone marrow, blood, or platelets, if needed." Tim attended a healing service and was prayed over in several different churches, as well as by his in-laws, the Spierenburgs, in a ceremony Jerry had written. He felt ready for whatever suffering lay ahead.

But Tim could hardly have imagined what was about to happen. Although his insurance company accepted the use of Interleukin, they declined to pay for the bone-marrow transplant, stating that it would probably not eliminate Tim's cancer. His physicians argued otherwise, saying his odds of going into remission were at least 30 to 40 percent. The insurers agreed to a further review. But this could take months, and a positive outcome was far from certain.

"This was the darkest hour," he says. "And yet, everywhere I looked, people were still praying and helping. A lawyer offered to fight the insurance company for me, pro bono. My business partner wanted to help me pay for the transplant. I felt God's presence in a close, tangible way—my faith had awakened, and an enormous amount of spiritual healing had taken place in my life. We decided to stick to our end-of-October schedule, try to pay for everything on our own, place ourselves in Jesus' hands, and await his will on this whole matter."

In October, Tim's mother-in-law returned to Bradenton for a few days to take care of some business matters because she knew they would have to stay in River Forest for an unspecified period of time. On Wednesday night at their church, Jackie ran into Sue Young. Sue had three ten-year-old girls from the SWAT team with her. "How is your son-in-law doing?" Sue asked.

Jackie explained the situation. "We're very concerned," she said.

Sue looked thoughtful. "The children here should be praying about this," she said, beckoning to the three girls. Quickly she explained Tim's situation.

The children pondered. "Let's pray that the cancer will dry up and go away," said one.

Another nodded. "Then the doctors won't have to do this awful thing, so the insurance company won't have to pay."

The third smiled and put her head back. "I can hear the doctor saying right now, 'Tim, why are you even here?'"

How simple. The children prayed as they had learned to do, commanding the tumor to leave. "Dry up and go away!" each one said. The entire SWAT team continued to pray for Tim's healing through the rest of the month.

At the end of October, although his case was on appeal, the insurance company was remaining firm in its decision: Tim would have to pay for his own bone-marrow treatment. The doctors told him that before they could go ahead, they must re-run tests to see how far the cancer had progressed during the past month. Tim's wife, Jan, was not enthused. "I hate to see you going through that again," she told him. But all those prayers rising on his behalf . . . Tim had experienced God's love and care in so many ways lately. *What harm would it do,* he thought, *to see if heaven had changed anything?*

After his tests, it was a while before the technician came out to the waiting room. When he did, he seemed a bit mystified. "Have you had any chemo treatments since the last time we did these tests?" he asked.

"None," Tim assured him. "Why?"

"Because . . ." the tech hesitated, "you seem to be in remission."

"But . . . ," Tim was elated. The prayers had been answered!

How could a chest tumor just disappear? Was there a mistake?

It was not there. When Tim's surgeon saw the test results, he canceled the bone-marrow transplant. "There isn't any cancer, Tim. None. Go home and enjoy it." He had no explanation for what had happened, he said, nor did any colleagues with whom he had discussed the case. As the children in Florida had requested, the tumor simply "blew away."

It has been nine years now, and Tim receives only an annual physical; no sign of his cancer has ever returned. His spiritual faith has blossomed. Tim is currently studying for his master of divinity degree at the University of Chicago's Divinity School and completing an internship at Christ Church in Oak Brook, Illinois. "Regardless of what the future holds, God has enriched and blessed my life and my spirit beyond measure," he says. "I have become a witness to his glory."

Children's prayer teams inspired by SWAT continue to form and have spread to other countries too. "God is moving powerfully worldwide, with children, teens, and adults. He is not leaving anyone out," Helen says. But children have that simple faith quality; they believe and are ready to act on their beliefs, she says, just as they did for Tim Holmes. "I believe they will have a great part in the coming revival."

MOMENTS OF LOVE

Coincidence is God's way of remaining anonymous.

—UNKNOWN

Grace Douvres grew up on a farm in Cornwall, England, where being with the animals was the best part of her life. But her career ultimately brought her to New York City, far from the green hills and hedgerows she had taken for granted for so long. Life in New York was exciting, especially after she met and married her husband, Jim, but she still missed her "critters."

One evening Jim came home from work with what appeared to be a lump under his overcoat. Grace was curious. "What have you got there?"

Jim grinned as he withdrew a tiny kitten, frail, dirty, and mewing plaintively. "She followed me upstairs from the subway," he explained sheepishly.

"Oh!" Grace was overjoyed. This was the cutest, sweetest, most adorable kitten she had ever seen. Or she would be, just as soon as Grace gave her a bath and nursed her back to health.

"We named her Bonnie because she was such a little 'bonnie belle' of a cat," Grace recalls. "Every day she grew more precious, and delighted us with her antics. I thanked God again and again for sending the perfect little companion for me." And as if Grace wasn't already pleased enough, Jim brought another kitten home one evening during a raging snowstorm.

"I think a neighbor abandoned him," Jim explained. "I couldn't leave him out there to starve, could I?"

"Of course not." Privately, Grace wondered if their home would soon become an animal shelter, but Jim apparently felt that two cats were enough. The second, named Heathcliff, settled in quickly. But despite her affection for him, Grace loved Bonnie best.

As Christmas approached that year, Grace began to notice advertisements for people to become foster parents to a child in a poverty-stricken area of the world. "Adopting" such a child meant sending a certain amount of money each month to ensure that the child would receive food, clothing, and an education. The child's guardian, in turn, would send a report on the child a few times each year. The idea appealed to Grace. She researched several organizations and decided on the one she would like to join. But life was busy, and the application remained on her desk.

One morning Grace noticed that Heathcliff seemed lethargic. He refused his food, ignored his toys, and, by evening, seemed terribly ill. "It sounds like feline leukemia," the veterinarian told Grace when she phoned. "You'd better bring him in first thing in the morning."

"Oh, no!" Grace knew what that meant. There was no cure for this virus, and cats with it were usually put to sleep right away, to spare them the pain associated with it. She would have to give consent for that, if necessary, to spare Heathcliff any more suffering.

The following morning Jim took Heathcliff to the veterinarian. The cat never returned. "Be careful," the vet warned Jim. "Not only is this illness fatal, it's also highly contagious."

Bonnie. Had she caught it from Heathcliff? Grace worried all day.

Within the week, Bonnie was exhibiting the same symptoms Heathcliff had. She was sluggish, had no appetite, and was not interested in things around her. Grace was devastated. She had little doubt that her cuddly companion had caught the fatal virus from Heathcliff. She would have to have her pet put to sleep. There wasn't any other choice.

Except . . . she could *pray* for a healing for Bonnie. She did. "It was a very tearful and apologetic prayer, because for some reason I felt guilty about asking God to heal a cat."

As she prayed, she noticed the foster-parent application on the desk. "I'll mail this tomorrow," she promised God, "so I can take care of someone like I'm asking you to take care of Bonnie. And if you do heal her, will you send me a sign that it wasn't a coincidence, that it really came from you?"

The following morning, Grace was amazed to see Bonnie pitter-patter over to her food dish and whine to be fed. A few hours later, she was throwing her rubber mouse in the air. "Jim!" Grace called. "I think Bonnie is getting well!"

Although it was never determined that Bonnie had feline leukemia, she did recover completely and was never sick again. Was God responsible for this? Grace remembered the "sign" she had requested when she prayed for her cat's recovery. It came a few weeks later, from the foster-parent organization.

"Thank you for becoming a foster parent," the letter read. "We have assigned you a little boy from the Philippine Islands. His name is Bonnie Sotio."

"This event comes under the heading of the 'wonders' of God, I think," says Grace. "Not terribly dynamic or startling, but just another indication of the love our Father has for us."

Sometimes God has to specifically rearrange his own natural order—time, space, nature—for something to be accomplished. As always, we are left with minds boggled.

For example, about six months before Betty Trotter's mother, Eileen Post, was diagnosed with Alzheimer's disease, Betty decided to arrange for Eileen to come from her home in Omaha to Betty's house in Chicago for a visit. Eileen had already shown some signs of vagueness, and Betty was uneasy about the whole trip. But there was no one in Omaha she could ask to oversee the plans. She would have to make the arrangements herself, pray about everything, and trust that God would go along on the trip.

Betty booked Eileen on a flight due to land at Chicago's O'Hare Airport about 3:00 p.m. on Wednesday. But on Wednesday morning snow began to fall. When Betty called O'Hare, she learned that her mother's flight had been canceled.

How was her mother, increasingly forgetful, going to understand this? "It took a great deal of patience, repetition over the telephone, and assistance from a local travel agent before Mom understood that she was to take the same flight the next day," says Betty. On Thursday morning, taking no chances, Betty phoned her mother again. "Are you ready to go to the airport, Mom?" she asked.

Eileen was confused. "Airport? Isn't that on Friday?"

Betty's heart sank. This was going to be harder than she'd hoped. "No, Mom. Remember, the plane was canceled yesterday. You're supposed to take the same flight today. And you need to be ready to go soon."

"Well . . . all right."

However, when Betty phoned back, about thirty minutes before her mother was to leave for the airport, Eileen was still vague. Was the trip today? No, she hadn't made transportation plans for getting to the airport. No, she hadn't packed. Concerned, Betty convinced her mother to go anyway. Once Eileen was at the airport, perhaps Betty could work out something with the airlines.

Betty hung up and started to pray. "God, I've got to have some help with Mother. Obviously, she's going to miss this flight now, but can you get her on the next? Please watch over her, and bring her here safely." Then she called her travel agent.

"Don't worry," said the agent. "I'll call the Omaha airport and tell them to find her and get her on the next flight; it lands at O'Hare about 4:00 p.m."

Betty hoped everything would work out. She ran a quick errand, got to the airport gate at 3:30—and stopped, dumbfounded. The 4:00 flight wasn't in yet. But her mother was sitting there calmly, waiting for her.

Betty found Eileen's suitcases stowed in an area away from the other baggage. Later, she learned that her husband had received a phone call from someone identifying himself as an airline representative, saying Eileen had been found wandering, disoriented, through the O'Hare terminal and was being brought to the gate where Betty had planned to meet her.

Everything had worked out—everything except the timing. For how did Eileen get on the earlier flight—with luggage packed—when she had been completely unprepared just before it left? And had she even been *on* that flight, considering the time she presumably wandered O'Hare's labyrinthine corridors before someone spotted her, found her son-in-law's phone number among her possessions, stowed her luggage in an out-of-the-way place, and brought her to the correct waiting area?

"We never discovered how Mother got here, and she didn't remember any of it," Betty says. But God protected her, just as Betty had asked.

Vincent Tan was born Tan Ban Soon in Singapore to Chinese Buddhist parents. As a young boy, Vincent was very interested in science. One day, as he read a book on nuclear physics in the library, he discovered an offer for a Bible course stuck within the pages of the book. Curious, Vincent ordered the course. Ultimately, he became a Christian, and because he wanted to attend a Christian college, he came to the United States and gave himself the Western name Vincent.

Vincent graduated from college and took a job in analytic chemistry in Chattanooga, Tennessee. His faith deepened, possibly because he wasn't afraid to share it with others, and life settled down. In March 1993, Vincent was working late in his lab, looking out the window occasionally to keep an eye on his car, because recently several had been stolen from the area. He noticed a stranger standing on the passenger side of his car. The man was young and clean-cut, but thieves come in all guises, and because Vincent is proficient in martial arts, he decided to investigate. Grabbing a long metal rod from the lab, he opened the door and called, "Yes? Can I help you?"

"Hi, Vincent," the stranger responded.

Vincent was startled. Had he mistaken a friend for a thief? No, he had never seen this man before. "Do I know you?" Vincent asked.

"Not really," the man responded. "But you don't have to use Chi Sao or the rod on me. And your mother is fine."

Now Vincent was really confused. No one in America knew of his skill in Chi Sao. Nor could the stranger see the rod Vincent held behind him. And who else could have known that his mother in China had just developed a heart problem?

The stranger smiled. "You love the Lord very much, don't you?"

"Yes, I do," Vincent answered. He started to relax.

"He loves you too," the man replied. "And he is coming very soon."

Vincent was thrilled. Could this be true? He looked away just for a second or two, and when he looked back, the man had disappeared.

Could he have been an angel? Eventually Vincent told his story to Jim Bramlett, an author who researches prophecies, and Jim used Vincent's experience, among others, in a magazine article.

Three years later, on Saturday, April 6, 1996, Vincent awoke at 4:30 a.m. with a strong belief that he was to pray. He wasn't exactly sure about *what,* but this urge had come upon him before, and he always had obeyed it. He prayed for a few moments, then fell asleep.

At 7:00 Vincent awakened again and began his usual morning prayer time. About a half hour later, his telephone rang. It was too early to answer the phone on a Saturday, he decided, and continued praying. The answering machine would handle the call.

But the phone kept ringing. Insistently. Had Vincent forgotten to turn on the answering machine? No, he could see the red light from where he knelt. Vincent got up and went to the phone. Ten rings, eleven . . . and although the caller ID was also turned on, no number was showing. Vincent gave up and grabbed the phone. "Hello?"

"Hello?" It was a woman's voice.

"Hello!" Vincent repeated.

"Hello!" the woman answered again.

"Yes—did you want to speak to me?" Vincent was getting exasperated.

"No."

"Then why did you call?"

"I didn't call," the woman answered, as annoyed as he. "*You* called me!"

Vincent explained that he hadn't—he had simply answered the phone. The very same thing had happened to the woman, whose name, she informed him, was Doris. "I live in Iowa," she said. "I can't imagine how this whole thing happened, Mr. . . . ?"

"My name is Vincent Tan," he answered politely, planning to say good-bye and end this strange mix-up. But the woman gave a little gasp.

"Are you the Vincent Tan who had an experience with an angel?"

"Well, yes."

"My mother and I read about it in a magazine. We never forgot what a wonderful story it was. Six months ago, my mother was diagnosed with terminal cancer. Every day since then, she has prayed that she might be able to speak with you before she died. This morning I awakened at 3:30, and I prayed, reminding the Lord of my mother's request."

Three thirty. Given the difference in time zones, Doris had awakened at the same moment as Vincent. They had been praying together.

"I can't believe this is happening," Doris went on. "Would it be too much to ask you to talk to my mother?"

"Put her on the phone," Vincent said.

The elderly lady's voice was weak and hardly audible, but for the next forty-five minutes or so, the two talked. Vincent told her about his angel experience in great detail, and they discovered that several of their favorite Scripture passages were the same. Finally, the elderly woman whispered, "Praise the Lord. Amen."

All became quiet. Thinking the old woman had fallen asleep, Vincent was about to hang up when Doris came back on the phone.

"Mother has died," she told Vincent. "Thank you for what you did for her."

Vincent was overwhelmed. A soul had just entered eternity, and he had been permitted to play a part in this joyous journey! He and Doris said their good-byes quickly so she could begin the necessary arrangements. It was not until several hours later that he realized he had never gotten Doris's last name or address, nor had the caller ID recorded her number. And Vincent never received a bill for the call, although Doris had told him she had answered *his* ring.

Vincent saw no point in investigating further, for the experience, he believes, was simply part of God's plan. "The Lord has his reasons for all of this," he says. "And as we near the final hours, I know that he is even closer."

When Mary McDonald (her name has been changed) learned that her daughter Sheila's father-in-law had died, she grabbed her car keys and went to the store to buy some food for the bereaved family. Who is ever prepared for out-of-town guests and neighbors coming by when something like this happens? "Sandra, our other daughter, made a huge salad and two chocolate pies," Mary recalls. "I bought a pan of frozen lasagna that's supposed to serve twelve not-very-big slices, and a smaller pan of macaroni and cheese, something that serves about eight or nine. I remember it specifically because I stood in the checkout line for a few moments wondering if it was enough. But I assumed other neighbors would be pitching in too."

When Mary and Sandra delivered their food, they were surprised to discover that it was all the grieving family had received. "I guess folks don't send food to bereaved families like they used to," Mary says. "There were nine people there—all extremely hungry and short on cash. They had enough to go downtown that evening and get hot dogs, which they did. I felt bad that I hadn't sent something for the next morning, because all they had were coffee cakes."

The next evening, however, the family (by now thirteen people) warmed the two pans. Sheila was there and witnessed everything. "It was strange, Mom," she told Mary later. "Some of these men are big eaters. But we not only didn't run out of lasagna and macaroni and cheese; there seemed to be a lot left over. Everyone said they were absolutely stuffed."

"Maybe someone else delivered the same thing," Mary suggested.

"No. I was in the kitchen. Your pans were the only ones there."

Mary hung up, briefly thinking of the miracle of the loaves and fish. But God didn't do things like that today, did he?

On the following day, the family got ready for the funeral and then had a small bite to eat. They ate from the same pans of lasagna and macaroni and cheese. The salad and pie had been long since consumed, but there was still plenty of the main course left. Everyone ate gratefully from overflowing plates again.

All this time Mary had been feeling a bit guilty about not bringing over more food. "But God never forgets," she says today. "He fills every need if we give him a little to work with."

Sometimes an angel's help is so gentle that we're apt to miss it if we aren't "tuned in." Cyril Phillips and his wife, Marjorie, live in the hilly outskirts of Kalamunda in Western Australia. Cyril sees his brother and sister-in-law, Mel and Flo, frequently, and Mel was always suggesting that the families take a vacation together. "I am not so keen on driving vacations," Cyril admits, "and as the Christmas holidays approached one year, and Mel began to really push about this, I became even firmer in my opposition."

While sawing wood one morning, Cyril heard a voice in his mind. "You are selfish," the voice said.

"It was an unexpected blow," Cyril says. "I was surprised and hurt." Cyril wondered if the voice was his angel's. "Why am I selfish?" he asked the voice.

"Marjorie and David would like to go on a trip," the voice said. Cyril felt sheepish and somewhat shocked. It had never occurred to him that his wife or son would enjoy traveling. But the next time Mel asked about the families sharing a vacation, Cyril said yes.

All arrangements were made, and the families met at Mel's house just as he was securing an oversize load with ropes on his large trailer. It was a beautiful day, but Cyril was a bit nervous about the size of Mel's trailer load—apparently his daughter, her husband, and their baby had decided to go too, with, of course, lots of extra supplies. Cyril believed in angels—hadn't one spoken to him about this event? He would just have to put the trip into their hands.

The two vehicles pulled out, and for a while everything went smoothly as they skirted around the suburbs and eventually reached the highway. "This is so relaxing," Marjorie told Cyril. "I'm glad we decided to go." She settled back again but a few moments later leaned forward. "Cyril," she asked, "do you smell burning rubber?"

Cyril looked at Mel's car, some distance ahead. "I was horrified to see a back wheel of the trailer actually flapping wildly about," Cyril recalls. Cyril caught up to Mel and motioned him over.

Mel's smile faded when he got out and saw the wheel. Immediately, he jacked up the trailer and pulled the wheel off. The men turned pale. Because the trailer's load had been so heavy, the thread grooves at the end of the axle had been stripped. The bolt would no longer hold the wheel onto the axle, even if they replaced it with their spare tire. There was no way they could drive any farther.

Cyril looked around. They were in a little-traveled area, deep in the bush. No houses were visible, and no one could remember when they had last passed one. They had a baby with them, and a child. It was getting later in the day. Cyril was standing behind Mel. All of a sudden he heard a voice in his head, the same voice he had heard once before. "Mel wants a piece of tinfoil."

Cyril looked around. No one had heard the voice but him. But even if it was something he should pay attention to, what were the chances of finding tinfoil out here? And what good would a thing like that do anyway? What they needed was a new axle.

But Cyril had been a friend of God's long enough to know that he could ask him for just about anything. "God," he said silently, "if there's tinfoil out here, and you have a plan for it and us, please show me where it is."

Almost immediately, as if he was being directed, Cyril walked diagonally across the road, stopped among the dry leaves, and picked up a piece of tinfoil that lay there, all by itself, in plain view. "Here's your tinfoil, Mel." He handed the item to his brother.

Mel's jaw dropped. "Where did you get *that*?" he asked. "I was just thinking that if I could wrap two pieces of tinfoil around the bolt, it would probably hold long enough to get us to a repair station. But who could find tinfoil here in the wilderness? What a wonderful coincidence!"

Not if you're listening to those small voices, Cyril thought as he watched his brother fix the wheel. Once again he thanked the angel who had told him he was selfish. "The incident made a profound impact on all of us, and my faith was greatly strengthened by it," he says today.

Seventh-grader Michael Halas had always enjoyed good health, so when he began running one fever after another, his parents were concerned. Then during one fever, Michael had joint pain as well. His father, John, remembered reading some articles about a newly discovered illness, Lyme disease, that had recently become more prevalent in their Voorhees, New Jersey, community. The symptoms of Lyme disease mimicked those of many other diseases, including juvenile rheumatoid arthritis. Some patients became very ill, or even permanently disabled, if the disease was not caught in its early stages. "Could this be Lyme disease?" John Halas asked the pediatrician the next time Michael ran a fever and went into the office.

"Not a chance," she answered without hesitation. "It's just a typical adolescent virus."

The Halas family had great confidence in this doctor, so they hated to argue. "But I remember reading something about joint pain being a symptom of Lyme," John persisted.

"It accompanies viruses too," the doctor assured him. The family went home. On the one hand, they were grateful that the doctor seemed so positive, and Michael would be spared such a serious sickness. But John had trouble sleeping that night. What if they were all wrong?

A few days later, for reasons now forgotten, John Halas and his wife exchanged cars. John traveled over one of the Delaware River bridges into Philadelphia from South Jersey. Returning to Jersey later than afternoon, he saw a piece of paper fly across the hood of the car and wedge itself under the edge. "It kept flapping like it was waving to me," John says. He sped up, trying to dislodge it, but with no success. The bothersome item hung on for the next fifteen miles, until John was able to get back to his office, park, and get out to see what it was.

The paper was actually a pamphlet of about ten pages, open in the middle, with one half wedged under the rim of the car's hood so perfectly that it looked as if it had been placed there by someone. Moreover, it was too thick to have stuck under the hood of his own car, had he been driving it that day. John took the pamphlet out, turned it over, and looked at the title. It was a booklet on Lyme disease.

"I ran to my office and read the booklet from cover to cover," John says. "I then phoned my wife, told her what happened, and we set off for the doctor's office. I didn't tell the doctor about the booklet then; we just said we wanted a Lyme test done ASAP." The doctor agreed, and the family had the results in about three days. The test was positive.

"Michael went on medication for the next thirty days, and the Lyme disease cleared up," John says. "We had caught it in time. Today he is healthy, strong, and healed."

Was it just a "coincidence" that the medical knowledge this family needed was provided to them in such a unique way? You decide.

HEAVEN IN HAZARD

Whatever we leave to God, God does
And blesses us.
—HENRY DAVID THOREAU, *INSPIRATION*

Ken Gaub grew up in Yakima, Washington, the oldest of six and the son of a man who had no use for God. But over the years, Ken's parents developed a deep spiritual faith. "I began to see amazing miracles and answers to prayer in my parents' lives," Ken says, "and I knew it had to be because of their commitment to God."

That was fine for them, but not for Ken. Oh, at times he'd practice preaching—"I'd get wound up and do a lot of hellfire and brimstone"—but Ken hoped someday to be a professional comedian. He had a gift for making people laugh, and he was the life of the party. He didn't see how both vocations could exist side by side. By the time Ken reached his teens, he was also somewhat of a daredevil. But God always seemed to protect him.

For example, Ken had fixed up an old car and took it out for a test drive one afternoon. Faster and faster he drove, down a deserted road. The gas pedal was almost to the floor when Ken spotted a large cardboard box lying ahead of him in the middle of the road. He would hit it, he decided, and watch it explode all over the place.

"But just before I reached it, I felt the steering wheel turning. The car was being taken out of my control, and somehow it went completely around the box, without touching it at all." Shocked, Ken looked in the rearview mirror and broke out in a cold sweat. Two little children were getting out of the box.

Ken knew that God had intervened in this situation. He was grateful but still not convinced that he was being called to the religious life. One night, however, Ken's father took the family to see a traveling minister conduct a religious revival in a tent. More than ten thousand people attended, and Ken was spellbound as miracle after miracle took place. On the way home, he announced to his parents, "Someday I'm going to do like that preacher. I'm going to have a tent and preach, and I'm going to help people just like he did."

It was certainly a worthy goal, but it took many years—and a lot of hardship and backsliding—before Ken began to see the beginnings of his dreams come true. He met his wife, Barbara, at Bible college in Washington, married her shortly before graduation, and decided they should leave for Kentucky. "Kentucky?" Barbara asked him. "Why there?"

Ken knew nothing about Kentucky except what he had seen in books. But his father had once lived there and had often described its beautiful mountains and creeks. "I think a lot of people need us there," Ken told her, so they loaded their old car with everything they owned and set out on their three-thousand-mile journey.

The couple evangelized their way across the country, "But either the people in those cities went to bed real early or they had other things to do," Ken says, because the couple's turnouts were small. What if they got to Kentucky and discovered that this was *not* the place where God intended them to go?

But when the Gaubs arrived in Hazard, Kentucky, they discovered that the people were hungry for education. Once Ken and Barbara found a place to live and a place where they could lead worship services, the neighbors came from all around Hazard to attend, sometimes walking for miles, barefoot despite the danger of snakes. Ken spent hours visiting the people up and down the creek and started a Bible school for the children. Money was always short, and Ken and Barbara lived on the edge most of the time, but God helped too. One day Ken had only one dollar for gasoline for his car. The attendant put in the dollar's worth, but when Ken pulled away, his tank was completely full. On other occasions, just as they spent the last of their money on food, someone would bring them something to eat. "We simply tried to obey the Lord and bless other people," Ken explains. "The more we blessed them, the more they blessed us."

But of course there were also people, as in any mission field, whose hearts were closed to the word of God. Ken usually respected their beliefs. And yet if someone in an unbelieving family was sick, it was hard for Ken not to visit, since praying for healing was, to him, one of the most important parts of his work. One day, he met Millie Johnson (her name has been changed) downtown. Millie's husband, Jake, a giant of a man, had told Ken in no uncertain terms several times just what he would do to him if he talked "that religion stuff" with Millie. But now Millie approached Ken with tears in her eyes. "Jeremy's very sick, Preacher," she said. "He's in the hospital." Jeremy was the Johnsons' one-year-old baby. "Do you think you could go and pray for him?"

"Millie, I'd be happy to go," Ken told her. "But you know how Jake feels about it."

"He's on a trip today," Millie said. "He'd never know."

"Okay." Ken had been heading to the hospital anyway, so he took some extra time to stop in Jeremy's room, lay hands on the baby, and pray for his recovery.

For the next week, each time he made his hospital rounds, Ken kept a lookout for Jake. If the man was visiting with his son, Ken bypassed the baby's room. If he saw Jake leaving, he knew he could stop to pray.

One particular day, the hallway outside Jeremy's room seemed exceptionally quiet.

Ken peeked in. No one was in the room, so he crept over to the crib where the baby lay covered with a sheet. Reaching out his hand, he softly touched the sheet covering Jeremy so as not to awaken him. "Lord," he prayed, "raise up this baby for your glory."

The baby started squirming. Ken decided he had better get out of there before little Jeremy cried and attracted attention. Just as Ken turned to leave, he saw that the doorway was blocked by Jake's very large frame. Jake was glaring at Ken.

"Now, Jake . . . ," Ken began.

Then Jake looked over at the crib and saw the sheet moving. "Oh, God! Oh, God!" he cried.

Ken tried to think of something to say to placate Jake and get around him. By now Jake's yelling had attracted a nurse. "Please, sir, this is a hospital," she said to Jake. "Calm down. I realize this is hard on you, but—"

Jake continued to yell and point at the crib. Then the nurse looked at the crib, and she screamed. All the color faded from her face as she backed out the door and ran down the corridor. Jake ran over and picked up the child.

Ken was at a loss as to why everyone was so upset. Maybe the baby was dying. Obviously, Ken had made the situation worse, so he left quickly before anything else could happen.

When the hospital phoned later to say that the Johnsons wanted Ken to return, he assumed that little Jeremy had died—or he was going to be reprimanded for intruding. Not knowing what to expect, he arrived at the hospital and was flabbergasted when Jake rushed up and threw his arms around him. "Preacher, I want you to know I changed my mind about that religious stuff. I believe now!" He began weeping and couldn't say any more.

"What's going on?" Ken asked.

Millie looked at him, tears streaming down her cheeks. "Preacher, didn't you know that our Jeremy had died two hours before you prayed for him?"

"What?" Ken was stunned.

"They had pronounced him dead—they were just waiting for Jake to have a last look at him."

"Well, I didn't know that," Ken explained. "I just felt I had to pray for that baby. I just asked God to raise him up for his glory."

"And God did?" Jake asked.

"We serve a wonderful God, Jake," Ken explained. His heart was full. God had certainly shown him that right here in Hazard, Kentucky, was where he wanted Ken and Barbara to be. And there would be no shortage of signs and wonders, as long as they placed their trust in him.

THE LAST WORD

These are the ones who have survived the time of great distress. . . .
[A]nd God will wipe away every tear from their eyes.

—Revelation 7:14, 17

Evelyn Heinz, a fellow writer and friend, told me an interesting story. She had become a grandmother again, this time to Victor Thomas, born December 27, 1997, in Colorado. Evelyn had been unable to be in Colorado for the birth but was hoping to travel there in March. In the meantime, she wrote a simple prayer asking that God would send angels to guard all her grandchildren, especially this latest addition.

"About a week after Victor's birth, my daughter Amy phoned to tell me that she and her husband, Craig, had taken the baby to their family physician for his first checkup," Evelyn told me. Baby Victor was sleeping contentedly on Craig's lap as they sat in the waiting room across from two elderly ladies, who were the only others there.

Suddenly Victor smiled in his sleep. Could it be a *real* smile, from a newborn? Amy and Craig stared. Yes, there it was again, and again.

Then one of the elderly ladies spoke, enthralled. "Look! There are angels all around your baby!"

It was just the answer Evelyn needed. "Since I couldn't be in Colorado yet, I believe God let me know he was watching over my grandchildren."

The reactions of everyone involved in this little episode were fascinating, I thought. If such a thing had happened in the 1980s, I suspect there might have been scoffing rather than acceptance. The elderly lady in the waiting room would have been regarded by the young couple as "slightly off." Evelyn might have not even thought to ask for angelic protection—or if she had, she might not have so matter-of-factly accepted her daughter's account as a tender and personal response from God.

But as we have seen in the preceding stories, angel sightings, visions, miracles, and answers to prayer are no longer considered rarities, limited to the experience of saints. God apparently is sending forth signs to everyone, all over the world. He wants us all to be part of his family.

That, of course, entails a decision. And God doesn't assure us of an easy journey, even if we do say yes. There will be rocky roads, valleys, confusion, occasional suffering. But God *does* pledge that he will always love us, and that he will be with us throughout it all.

What a promise! The King of kings, the great I Am, the Alpha and Omega, the God of Abraham, Isaac, and Jacob, who threw the planets into the skies, who split the Red Sea and carved the mountains out of the earth . . .

. . . loves *you*.

Hold out your arms. Close your eyes. Open your heart and invite him in. Finally. Forever.

Whatever happens, life will never be the same again.

Recommended Reading List

Brown, Michael. *The Final Hour*. Milford, OH: Faith Publishing, 1992.

————. *The Trumpet of Gabriel*. Milford, OH: Faith Publishing, 1994.

Connell, Janice T. *Meetings with Mary: Visions of the Blessed Mother*. New York: Ballantine Books, 1995.

McAll, Kenneth. *Healing the Family Tree*. London: Sheldon Press, 1999.

Miller, Duane. *Out of the Silence: A Personal Testimony of God's Healing Power*. With Gary Thomas. Nashville: Thomas Nelson, 1996.

OTHER AREAS OF INTEREST

Angel Network Charities, 5339 Kalanianaole Highway, Honolulu, HI 96821; phone: (808) 373-4998, (808) 377-1841; fax: (808) 373-7233.

The Padre Pio Foundation of America, 463 Main Street, Cromwell, CT 06416; phone: (860) 635-4996; fax: (860) 635-PPIO (7746); e-mail: padrepio@padrepio.com.

SWAT staff members are available to come and train other church staffs. Contact Helen Beason, P.O. Box 105, Litchfield, IL 62056; (217) 324-2899.

If you would like Ken Gaub to speak at your church or event, contact him at Ken Gaub Ministries, P.O. Box 1, Yakima, WA 98907; phone: (509) 575-1965; fax: (509) 575-4732; e-mail: kengaub@aol.com

Angels on Earth magazine, *Guideposts,* P.O. Box 39, Seminary Hill Road, Carmel, NY 10512; www.guideposts.org.

SHARE YOUR STORY

I am always interested in hearing from readers who would like to share their angel encounters, miracles, answers to prayer, and other heavenly wonders. Please write to me at P.O. Box 127, Prospect Heights, IL 60070. Or you can e-mail me at joan@joanwanderson.com or visit my Web site at http://www.joanwanderson.com.

If I can use your story in my future writing, I will contact you for permission.

Joan Wester Anderson

About the Author

Joan Wester Anderson is the best-selling author of *Where Angels Walk, Where Miracles Happen, Where Wonders Prevail, An Angel to Watch Over Me,* and *In the Arms of Angels.* Her work, totaling fifteen books and more than a thousand articles and stories, has been widely published in newspapers and in such magazines as *Reader's Digest, Woman's Day,* and *Modern Bride.* The author has appeared on *Oprah, Good Morning America, NBC Nightly News,* the Eternal Word Television Network, and many other national and local shows and has been featured on several videos dealing with angels and miracles. She and her husband live in a Chicago suburb. They have five grown children and two grandchildren.

Join In. Speak Up. Help Out!

Would you like to help yourself and the greater Catholic community by simply talking about Catholic life and faith? Would you like to help Loyola Press improve our publications? Would you be willing to share your thoughts and opinions with us in return for rewards and prizes? If so, please consider becoming one of our **special Loyola Press Advisors.**

Loyola Press Advisors is a unique online community of people willing to share with us their perspectives about Catholic life, spirituality, and faith. From time to time, registered advisors are invited to participate in brief online surveys and discussion groups. As a show of our gratitude for their service, we recognize advisors' time and efforts with **gift certificates, cash, and other prizes.** Membership is free and easy. We invite you, and readers like yourself, to join us by registering at www.SpiritedTalk.org.

Your personal information gathered by SpiritedTalk.org is stored in a protected, **confidential** database. Your information will never be sold to or shared with another third party! And SpiritedTalk.org is for research purposes only; at no time will we use the Web site or your membership to try to sell you anything.

Once you have registered at SpiritedTalk.org, every now and then you will be invited to participate in surveys—most take less than ten minutes to complete. Survey topics include your thoughts and ideas regarding the products and services you use in relation to Catholic life and spiritual growth. You may also have the opportunity to evaluate new Loyola Press products and services before they are released for sale. For each survey you complete, you will earn gift certificates, points, or prizes! Membership is voluntary; you may opt out at any time.

Please consider this opportunity to help Loyola Press improve our products and better serve you and the greater Catholic community. We invite you to visit **www.SpiritedTalk.org,** take a look, and register today!

Also Available

by Joan Wester Anderson

In the Arms of Angels: True Stories of Heavenly Guardians
ISBN 0-8294-2040-1 • 7-5/16" x 7-7/16" Paperback
292 pages • $14.95

Do you believe in angels? You will after reading *New York Times* best-selling author Joan Wester Anderson's latest collection of extraordinary stories of angelic encounters. From a harrowing story of a World Trade Center survivor to the heartrending tale of a little boy who miraculously survives a horrible car crash, Joan Wester Anderson brings together some of the most compelling true stories of angelic appearances from the last five years. *In the Arms of Angels* is inspiring evidence of the heavenly guardians who stand always at the ready to guide and protect us—and offer each of us a glimpse of eternity.

Available through your favorite bookstore, or call **800.621.1008** or visit **www.Loyolabooks.org** to order.